OLD TESTAMENT MESSAGE

A Biblical-Theological Commentary

Carroll Stuhlmueller, C.P. and Martin McNamara, M.S.C.
EDITORS

Old Testament Message, Volume 12

ISAIAH 40-66

John Scullion, S.J.

Michael Glazier, Inc.
Wilmington, Delaware

First published in 1982 by: MICHAEL GLAZIER, INC. 1723 Delaware Avenue, Wilmington, Delaware 19806
Distributed outside U.S., Canada & Philippines by: GILL & MACMILLAN, LTD., Goldenbridge, Inchicore, Dublin 8 Ireland

Library of Congress Catalog Card Number: 82-081224
International Standard Book Number
Old Testament Message series: 0-89453-235-9
ISAIAH 40-66
0-89453-246-4 (Michael Glazier, Inc.)
7171-1176-8 (Gill & MacMillan, Ltd.)

Cover design by Lillian Brulc

Typography by Susan Pickett

Printed in the United States of America

Contents

Chapters 56-66

Editors' Preface

Old Testament Message brings into our life and religion today the ancient word of God to Israel. This word, according to the book of the prophet Isaiah, had soaked the earth like "rain and snow coming gently down from heaven" and had returned to God fruitfully in all forms of human life (Isa 55:10). The authors of this series remain true to this ancient Israelite heritage and draw us into the home, the temple and the marketplace of God's chosen people. Although they rely upon the tools of modern scholarship to uncover the distant places and culture of the biblical world, yet they also refocus these insights in a language clear and understandable for any interested reader today. They enable us, even if this be our first acquaintance with the Old Testament, to become sister and brother, or at least good neighbor, to our religious ancestors. In this way we begin to hear God's word ever more forcefully in our own times and across our world, within our prayer and worship, in our secular needs and perplexing problems.

Because life is complex and our world includes, at times in a single large city, vastly different styles of living, we have much to learn from the Israelite Scriptures. The Old Testament spans forty-six biblical books and almost nineteen hundred years of life. It extends through desert, agricultural and urban ways of human existence. The literary style embraces a world of literature and human emotions. Its history began with Moses and the birth-pangs of a new people, it came of age politically and economically under David and Solomon, it reeled under the fiery threats of prophets like Amos and Jeremiah. The people despaired and yet were re-created with new hope during the Babylonian exile. Later reconstruction in the homeland and then the trauma of apocalyptic movements prepared for the revelation of "the mystery hidden for ages in God who created all things" (Eph 3:9).

While the Old Testament telescopes twelve to nineteen hundred years of human existence within the small country of Israel, any single moment of time today witnesses to the reenactment of this entire history across the wide expanse of planet earth. Each verse of the Old Testament is being relived somewhere in our world today. We need, therefore, the *entire* Old Testament and all twenty-three volumes of this new set, in order to be totally a "Bible person" within today's widely diverse society.

The subtitle of this series—"A Biblical-Theological Commentary"—clarifies what these twenty-three volumes intend to do.

Their *purpose* is theological: to feel the pulse of God's word for its *religious* impact and direction.

Their *method* is biblical: to establish the scriptural word firmly within the life and culture of ancient Israel.

Their *style* is commentary: not to explain verse by verse but to follow a presentation of the message that is easily understandable to any serious reader, even if this person is untrained in ancient history and biblical languages.

Old Testament Message—like its predecessor, *New Testament Message*—is aimed at the entire English-speaking world and so is a collaborative effort of an international team. The twenty-one contributors are women and men drawn from North America, Ireland, Britain and Australia. They are scholars who have published in scientific journals, but they have been chosen equally as well for their proven ability to communicate on a popular level. This twenty-three book set comes from Roman Catholic writers, yet, like the Bible itself, it reaches beyond interpretations restricted to an individual church and so enables men and women rooted in biblical faith to unite and so to appreciate their own traditions more fully and more adequately.

Most of all, through the word of God, we seek the blessedness and joy of those

who walk in the law of the Lord!...
who seek God with their whole heart (Ps. 119:1-2).

Carroll Stuhlmueller, C.P.   *Martin McNamara, M.S.C.*

INTRODUCTION

1. Historical Background

A) JERUSALEM AND JUDAH

It was Nebuchadnezzar, ruler 605-562, who established the supremacy of the Babylonian empire after the final destruction of the Assyrian empire and army in 609, and the defeat of the Egyptians at Carchemish on the Euphrates in 605. After succeeding his father as king, Nebuchadnezzar returned to Syria-Phoenicia and drove the Egyptians slowly southwards in a series of campaigns 603-602, but was unsuccessful in his attempt to invade Egypt in 601.

This failure tempted Jehoiakim of Jerusalem whose submission to Nebuchadnezzar had lasted three years to withhold tribute. Nebuchadnezzar could not for the moment deal with Jehoiakim's insubordination, but tribes loyal to him, Syrians, Moabites, Ammonites, harrassed Jerusalem. It was not until 598-597 that the Babylonians could turn to the siege of Jerusalem. Jehoiakim died three months before the surrender of the city under his son and successor Jehoiachin who was duly taken off to Babylon, 2 Kgs 24. This was the first of the deportations. The king, royal family, the nobles and some ten thousand from the warriors and craftsmen were removed and settled in Babylon, 2 Kgs 24:8-16; 2

Chr 36:9-10. The deuteronomistic historian tells us that "none remained, except the poorest people of the land," 2 Kgs 24:14.

The Babylonians installed a new king whose throne name was Zedekiah, originally Mattaniah, a son of Josiah and uncle of his young predecessor Jehoiachin. It was Zedekiah's revolt some ten years later in 587-586 that brought the supreme penalty on Jerusalem. The walls were thrown down, the temple was razed and its sacred vessels were carried off, the city was destroyed throughout, 2 Kgs 25:1-21. There seems to have been large scale deportation, "but the captain of the guard left some of the poorest of the land to be vine-dressers and ploughmen," 2 Kgs 25:11-12.

While the evidence for the destruction of the city is beyond dispute, that for the number of deportees causes difficulties. The Second Book of Kings gives both ten thousand and seven thousand plus one thousand for the deportation of 598-597, 2 Kgs 24:14, 16. This seems to be a round number. Jeremiah 52:28-30 gives three thousand twenty three. For the deportations the Book of Kings records that ". . . the rest of the people who were left in the city and the deserters who had deserted to the king of Babylon, together with the rest of the multitude, Nebuzaradan the captain of the guard carried into exile," 2 Kgs 25:11. Jeremiah gives the number as eight hundred and thirty two. He also records a third deportation of seven hundred and forty five in the year 582 which is not mentioned in the Book of Kings. The total number of deportees according to Jeremiah 52:28-30 was four thousand six hundred, a figure considerably less than that of 2 Kgs 24-25. The rather modest and precise numbers given by Jeremiah together with the introductory sentence, "This is the number of the people whom Nebuchadnezzar carried away captive," Jer 52:28, would indicate that he was preserving an extract from an official record. One must remember too the oriental custom of enumerating a population: the men were counted, the women and children were not included.

There seems to be no way of explaining the disparity in

the figures of Kings and Jeremiah though W. F. Albright had noted that "the difference may be partly due to the heavy mortality of the starving and diseased captives during the long trek to Babylonia." Modern scholars are not at one as to the number removed from Judah to Babylonia under Nebuchadnezzar: one has proposed not less than fourteen or fifteen thousand (C.F. Whitely); another some eighteen thousand (R.H. Pfeiffer); yet a third about five thousand men increased to not more than twenty thousand with women and children (K. Galling). The constant and well attested Assyrian practice of depopulating by simple transfer of people, the biblical evidence of 2 Kgs 24-25 and Jer 52:28-30, as well as the extra-biblical evidence all point to the removal of a substantial and notable portion of the people of Judah. To this may be added the archaeological evidence which, though sparse, confirms widespread destruction of Judean towns in the early part of the sixth century.

After the year 587-586 the situation in Jerusalem-Judah was as follows: the city of Jerusalem was in ruins, the walls were down, the Temple was razed with no prospect of rebuilding; the upper and influential classes had been deported together with an appreciable number of craftsmen who with their skills might otherwise furnish the means of revolt; the cities of Judah had been by and large destroyed, but the peasant population seems to have remained. Albrecht Alt has shown clearly that the deportations under Nebuchadnezzar were not strict deportations in the Assyrian sense of the word. Nebuchadnezzar did not settle people from other parts of the Neo-Babylonian empire on Judean soil, nor did he make the now small Jerusalem area a separate Babylonian province with its own organization. He put Jerusalem under the administration of the governor of Samaria. Alt concludes that the measures taken by Nebuchadnezzar were no more than half measures. There is much truth in this. But the half measures were very effective.

Some two centuries later the Chronicler portrayed the course of events from the destruction of Jerusalem to the return after the edict of Cyrus in such a way as to suggest that the real history of Jerusalem should be traced through the captivity and the returned exiles. Martin Noth has issued a caution here. He insists that though this line of continuity is important, it is one-sided. The Babylonian group did influence the whole history of Israel; nevertheless it "represented a mere outpost, whereas Palestine was and remained the central area of Israel's history, and the descendants of the old tribes who remained in the land, with the holy place of Jerusalem, constituted not only numerically the great mass but also the real nucleus of Israel." But Noth's judgment too must be counter-balanced by the evidence from Jeremiah. Even before the deportations of 587-586 "the king of Babylon slew all the nobles of Judah," Jer 39:6. Nebuzaradan the captain of the guard "carried into exile to Babylon the rest of the people who were left in the city, those who had deserted to him, and the people who remained," Jer 39:6. And in the following verse we read that this same Nebuzaradan "left in the land of Judah some of the poor people who owned nothing, and gave them vineyards and fields at the same time." Jeremiah says twice that only the poorest of the land were left, 40:7; 52:15-16. It was a remnant, 40:11.

Even if Jeremiah's words are a somewhat exaggerated melancholy reflection, yet they leave the impression that Jerusalem-Judah was greatly reduced in population. At the same time however under Gedaliah "...all the Jews who were in Moab and among the Ammonites and in Edom and in other lands...returned from all the places to which they had been driven and came to the land of Judah, to Gedaliah at Mizpah," Jer 40:11-12. Later, after the murder of Gedaliah, many of the leading men and their families went down to settle in Egypt, taking Jeremiah and Baruch with them, Jer 43:1-7. It is difficult to avoid the conclusion that materially Jerusalem-Judah was in a poor state in the years following 587-586, and that its population, notably depleted, was scarcely a vital and influential force. Some sort of sacrifice however does seem to have continued at the place where the Temple had been: "On the day after the murder of Gedaliah, before any one knew of it, eighty men arrived from Shechem and Shiloh and Samaria, with their beards shaved and their clothes torn, and their bodies gashed, bringing cereal offerings and incense to present at the temple of the Lord," Jer 41:4-5.

The deuteronomistic history comes to an end with the destruction of Jerusalem, and the evidence for conditions in Jerusalem during the fifty years 587-538 is practically zero.

B) BABYLON

(See Cyrus Cylinder, *ANET*, 315-316: Herodotus 1, 190)

When Babylon fell to Cyrus the Persian in October 539 Israel had been in captivity for just on fifty years. Many of the original captives had died; those taken captive in their 'teens and early twenties were now about the biblical age of three score and ten; a new generation had grown up around them which had never experienced Jerusalem and its temple, but had been exposed to life in Babylon and to the processions of the images of the Babylonian gods through the streets at New Year to the ziggurat of Marduk. This must have had its effect and a number must have been lured away from their true God. The general outlook was hopeless and there was no prospect of a return to Jerusalem. The Jews in Babylon were not persecuted; they were allowed to live their own lives, to follow their law, to come together and pray, though they had no temple, liturgy or system of sacrifice. Their lot was tolerable, insofar as a state of captivity can be tolerable. Still, there seemed to be no future.

C) CYRUS AND DELIVERANCE

Cyrus of Persia was the most effective leader in the middle east in the period 559-530. After establishing himself in Persia (modern province of Pars in the south of Iran) he gained control of Media in the north and took its capital Ecbatana (modern Hamadan) high up on the Zagros mountain range. Now master of the Medes and the Persians Cyrus moved west conquering Armenia, Cappadocia and Cilicia in what is now modern Turkey. Then in 547 he took Sardis the capital of Croesus' kingdom of Lydia (Herodotus 1; Narbonidus Chronicle, *ANET*, 306). Cyrus then moved back eastwards, conquered the remainder of Iran, and penetrated into south-west India. In the meantime the Babylonian empire was undergoing a process of internal decay.

The prophet of the exile, Second Isaiah, saw his God as Lord of history at work in these political movements. Cyrus, the military and political victor, was God's instrument which was to bring captive Israel back to Jerusalem and Judah. On the stage of world history the return was but an insignificant event, scarcely as much as a side-show; but in the prophet's perspective it was a mighty act of God which demanded language and imagery suited to such an event. Second Isaiah spoke his message in those ten years, more or less, which preceded Cyrus' bloodless entry into Babylon in October 539.

2. Second Isaiah

Up to the period of the Enlightenment in the 18th century it was accepted without question that the sixty six chapters of the biblical book of Isaiah were the work of the great prophet of that name in the last decades of the 8th century. In 1775 J. C. Döderlein in his commentary *Esaias* detached chaps. 40-66 from that period and set them in the period of the exile in the sixth century. Just over a century after Döderlein wrote, the separation of chaps. 40-66 had been accepted by critical scholars as an established result of critical scholarship so that in 1889 Franz Delitzsch, a conservative rather than a radical, could write in the fourth edition of his commentary that the chapters must be considered as a product of the exilic period. And Rudolf Kittel in his revision of August Dillmann's commentary in 1898 wrote that much as we may like to attribute chaps. 40-66 to

Isaiah of the 8th century, we cannot.

The reasons for separating chaps. 40-66 from chaps. 1-39 are always essentially the same and convincing: 1) *the historical background*: destruction, exile and suffering are presumed; there is familiarity with the history of the 6th century, above all with Cyrus, and firsthand experience of Babylonian religion; and a prophet speaks both out of and into the situation of his contemporaries. 2) *themes*: there are the themes of comfort and salvation, a new salvation under a new covenant; God is presented as creator and maker, and his action in history as redeemer and saviour is rooted in his action as creator. 3) *style and vocabulary*: chaps. 40-66 are more prolix; there is constant repetition and doubling of words; there is familiarity with the style of the psalms of descriptive praise with their heaping up of present participles; Jerusalem and objects are personified. These reasons have thoroughly convinced most scholars.

It was Bernhard Duhm in his commentary in 1892 (of which there were four editions, the last in 1922) who further divided what had by then become known as Second Isaiah. It is no exaggeration to say that his "conclusions" have determined the scholarly approach to Isaiah, especially to chaps. 40-66, up to the present day. Duhm says quite clearly, and quite correctly, that to establish the date and source of the individual pieces that go to make up the book of Isaiah we have to rely mainly on internal criticism, but that to maintain that the author of chaps. 40-66 was one and the same with the great realist of the 8th century, one would have to adopt a quite uncritical mentality. Duhm had already brought substantial sections of chaps. 1-39 down to the second half of the 2nd century (a view that cannot be sustained). Second Isaiah, which for Duhm comprised only chaps. 40-55, would have worked, spoken and written about 540. The servant songs (42:1-4; 49:1-6; 50:4-9; 52:13—53:12) are exceptions; they are post-exilic and were inserted into the text at a later date. (See Excursus 2, *The Problem of Servant Songs*, and the introduction to chaps. 56-66.)

3. The Speech of Second Isaiah

The prophet of the exile is in the best traditions of Israelite prophecy, prayer and liturgical life. Like the 8th century prophets and Jeremiah he at first shrinks from his calling. He calls doom; he is one with his sinful nation. He praises God in the traditional forms of prayer and is completely familiar with the prayer of the Psalter; in fact one cannot read three or four verses without meeting the language of the Psalter. Second Isaiah speaks promises or oracles (assurances) of salvation, 41:8-13, 14-16; 43:1-4, 5-7; 44:1-5, and makes proclamations of salvation, 41:17-20; 42:14-17; 43:16-21; 49:7-12. He is full of the language of praise, *e.g.*, 40:12-17; 44:24-28; he uses the language of the court for disputations or trial speeches: 41:1-5, 21-29; 43:8-15, 22-28; 44:6-8, 21-22; 45:20-25; he directs accusations against Israel: 42:18-25; 43:22-28; 50:1-3; he cries out in exultation: 42:10-12; 44:23; 45:8; 48:20; 49:13; 52:9-11; 54:1-2. Then there are the famous servant songs: 42:1-4; 49:1-6; 50:4-9; 52:13 - 53:12. The prophet takes up the traditional themes and imagery of the origins of the world and forges an indissoluble link between creation and God's action in history as redeemer; he sees the fulfillment of the divine purpose for his holy, covenanted, chosen, called, redeemed people in the movements started by Cyrus; he resumes prophecy as proclaimed by Jeremiah; he uses the traditional forms of judicial proceedings for judgments in the heavenly realm and on earth; he is steeped in the liturgical and prayer life of his people.

The prophet is both traditionalist and innovator: the traditionalist brings the theology and cultural heritage at hand to bear on his people who are once again to experience God's liberating action in history; the innovator reaches back beyond history into the eternity of God the creator so that God's redeeming action in history can be founded in creation which is the beginning of history. His whole theme from 40:1 to 55:13 is the creator God's saving action in history which is to bring Israel back to Jerusalem and give her a new destiny.

Some theological themes are treated in the Excursuses to the commentary on chaps. 40-55, others after chaps. 56-66. Most themes however are taken up as they occur in the text with references to parallel passages.

CHAPTERS 40-55

40:1-11.
THE FIRST WORDS OF CONSOLATION

40 Comfort, comfort my people, says your God;
[2]Speak to the heart of Jerusalem and tell her
that her warfare is ended
that her guilt is discharged
that she has received from the hand of Yahweh
double for all her sins.
[3]A voice is crying: prepare a way for Yahweh in the desert
erect a highway for our God in the wilderness.
[4]Every valley will be raised up,
every mountain and hill will be lowered.
The slopes will become flat and the steppes a plain.
[5]And the glory of Yahweh will be revealed
and all mankind will see his gaze,
for the mouth of Yahweh has spoken.
[6]A voice says: Cry! and I said, what shall I cry?
All flesh is grass, and all its constancy as the
flower of the field.
[7]The grass withers, the flower fades,
for the breath of Yahweh has blown on it (truly
the people is grass).
[8]The grass withers, the flower fades, but the word
of our God stands for ever.

[9]Up now on a mountain, Zion, messenger of good news,
raise your voice with strength, Jerusalem,
messenger of good news,
raise it, do not fear:
say to the cities of Judah: here is your God!
[10]See, Yahweh the Lord is coming with strength,
and his own might rules for him.
See, his reward is with him, yes, his prize before him.
[11]Like a shepherd he shepherds his flock,
he gathers them in his arms;
the lambs, yes, he lifts them in his bosom,
the ewes he leads to water.

(translation by author)

vv. 1-2. The prophet of the exile uses the image of the heavenly court and the God of Israel tells its members to comfort his people. The council of the gods of Canaan has left its print on the Hebrew Bible: 1 Kgs 22:19ff; Isa 6; Job 1-2; Pss 82(81):1; 89(88):7; Dan 7:9; Rev 4:1-11. The court is to speak effectively to Jerusalem, *i.e.* the people in exile rather than the city itself, to get through to her, to convince her. Deliverance and forgiveness go together. God turns again to his chosen people.

vv. 3-5. "A voice is crying" or, as R.N. Whybray has suggested, "Listen! someone is calling out." As Yahweh led his people out of Egypt through the desert of Sinai, so once more he is to lead them through a desert, out of Babylon through the Sinai desert. The second exodus is to outdo the first; the procession will be literally along a high way, a road rising up.

God in action will reveal his glory, or in Hebrew *kābôd*. In Babylon there were processions of the splendid images of the gods during the festivals, showing forth their glory. But Yahweh does not appear in visible form; his glory is shown by his action in history. Moses had asked: "I pray thee, show me thy glory. And he said. . . but you cannot see my face. . . there is a place by me where you shall stand upon the rock;

and while my glory passes by I will put you in a cleft of the rock, and I will cover you with my hand until I pass by... but my face shall not be seen," Exod 33:17-23; *cf.,* Isa 6; Ezek 11:22-23. The Second Isaiah uses *kābôd* only of Yahweh, 40:5; 42:8, 12; 43:7; 48:11. The author(s) of chaps. 56-66 uses it of Yahweh: 58:8; 59:19; 60:1, 2; of Zion: 62:2; 66:11; of the nations: 61:6; of Lebanon: 60:13. In Cana of Galilee God acting in Jesus "manifested his glory, and his disciples believed in him," Jn 2:11. When the "mouth of Yahweh has spoken," there is no more to be said. His word *is* effective action.

vv. 6-8. When a voice from the heavenly court says "Cry!" the prophet asks what is he to cry. Now is sounded a prophetic leitmotif — the inconstancy of humankind, and specifically of Israel, and the constancy of God. In the Middle East the spring flowers and the grass wither under the eastern sirocco; the grass on the mud roofs of the houses shows up fresh in the morning and lies dead by the afternoon, Ps 90(89):5-6. Such is the constancy, steadfast love, *hesed* (*not* glory or beauty as in RSV) of humankind, of Israel in all her weakness. Not so God. His constancy, steadfast love, is unfailing. It is typical of the prophet's style that he repeats the image symbolizing man's inconstancy in v. 8; BUT, "the word of our God stands for ever." The effectiveness of the divine word is best expressed in such passages as Isa 55:10-11; Ps 33(32):6, as well as in the creation-by-word in Gen 1.

The divine word in act has a long history in the ancient Near East. In Sumer in the 3rd millennium B.C. the god makes his voice or word known in the thunder, and an essential part of the whole idea complex is the "creative word." In Canaanite mythology from the 14th-13th century B.C. Baal, the storm god, creates the thunder and in it his word of command is heard, or rather it is his word of command. This is echoed throughout Ps 29(28). The Hebrew *dābār* means word and event; *dābār* had not been found in any other semitic language but Hebrew until the tablets from Ebla, Tell Mardikh, 60 km. s-w of Aleppo in Syria and from about 2200 B.C., discovered and published in the mid-70's, gave us *é-da-barki*, which may be rendered "temple of the word," a divinization of *dābār*, word (see comment on 55:10-11).

These and further references to the myths, symbols and texts from the ancient Near East are given so as to remind us that the text of the Hebrew Bible did not arise out of a vacuum, but is the heir of a long tradition of literature, imagery and thought patterns.

vv. 9-11. The prophet addresses not the exiles but Zion-Jerusalem who is to be the messenger of good news to the rest of Judah. It is the Lord, Yahweh himself, who is coming and he brings Israel with him. The action is wholly his; "his reward. . . his prize" is the people he brings back. Yahweh comes "with strength" v. 10, but also as a shepherd who cares both for the nation as a whole and for each individual. The image of the shepherd has a long history in the ancient Near East and beyond. A hymn to the Sun-God, Shamash, from the library of the Assyrian king Ashurbanipal, 668-633 B.C., reads:

> Whatever Ea, the counsellor king, has willed to create, thou art guarding altogether
> Those endowed with life, thou likewise dost tend;
> Thou indeed art their shepherd, both above and below.
> (*ANET*, 378, lines 24-26)

There is also the ancient oriental metaphor, "the king is the shepherd of his people." In Homer king Agamemnon is referred to some 18 times in the stock phrase "shepherd of the host (armies)," Iliad 2:772; 5:513, 573; 7:230; 11:202. . . . The image is traditional in Israel: Isa 63:14; Ezek 34:10ff; Pss 23(22):1, 79(78):13; 80(79):1; 95(94):7; 100(99):3. Yahweh is first of all the shepherd of his people, Israel.

40:12-31. GOD — IMMEASURABLE AND INCOMPARABLE

The centre of this passage is the immeasurability, the incomparability, the incomprehensibility, the inexhaustibility of God. If Yahweh, Israel's God, is the creator God, surely he can create his people anew and become their redeemer God. What are the gods of Babylon who may have beguiled some of the captive Israelites as they moved in spectacular procession along the streets of Babylon? They are nothing but the work of a craftsman or goldsmith! But Yahweh is the Lord of creation and so the Lord of history. The passage divides reality into four sections, vv. 12-17, 18-24, 25-26, 27-31 which, whatever may have been their pre-history, form here a literary unit, the work of Second Isaiah, who has impressed his theology and creative genius on whatever he has inherited, be it form or material. The questions in vv. 12-14, 18, 21, 25 are rhetorical; only v. 27 introduces a real "disputation" piece.

vv.12-17

> [12]Who has measured the sea in the hollow of his hand,
> has gauged the heavens with a span?
> [13]Who has gauged the mind of Yahweh,
> who was his counsellor, who guided him?
> [14]Who counselled him and instructed him,
> who taught him the way of order?
> who brought him experience,
> who guided him along the path of instruction?
> [15]Look! the nations are reckoned as but a drop from a bucket,
> as but dust on the scale pan.
> Look! the islands weigh as but fine dust!
> [16]Lebanon is not enought for burning,
> nor its animals for burnt offering.
> [17]All the nations are as nothing before him,
> reckoned as non-existent, emptiness by him.

(translation by author)

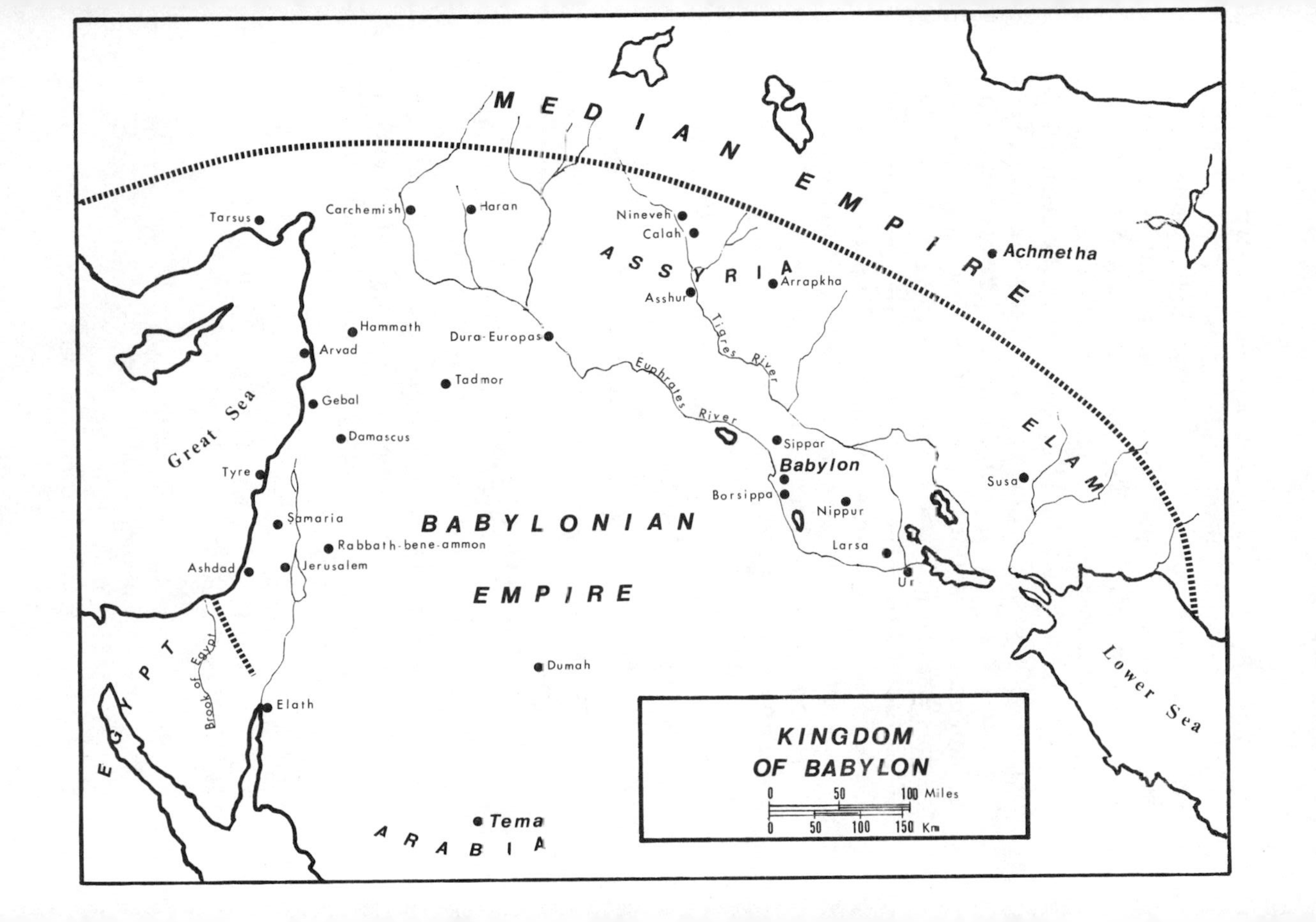
KINGDOM
OF BABYLON
0 50 100 Miles
0 50 100 150 Km
MEDIAN EMPIRE
Achmetha
ASSYRIA
Nineveh
Calah
Asshur
Arrapkha
Tigres River
Euphrates River
ELAM
Susa
Lower Sea
Sippar
Babylon
Borsippa
Nippur
Larsa
Ur
BABYLONIAN
EMPIRE
Tarsus
Carchemish
Haran
Hammath
Dura-Europas
Arvad
Tadmor
Gebal
Damascus
Great Sea
Tyre
Samaria
Rabbath-bene-ammon
Ashdad
Jerusalem
EGYPT
Brook of Egypt
Elath
Dumah
Tema
ARABIA

The passage is polemical. There was no struggle at the beginning between Yahweh and the primeval sea (or Yam = sea, a Cannanite monster), as there was in Babylonian myth between primeval Apsu (fresh water) and Tiamat (salt water), and no dividing of the monster Tiamat by Marduk to form the heavens and the earth out of her parts. Yahweh was the supreme master. The answer to all the questions is, of course, "no-one." He alone did it. It is not a question of "who is able. . . ," but of who did it all before history began. It happened in mythical time, before there was order or cosmos, because he alone was there, he "the eternal God," v. 28. Before Yahweh the immeasurable and incomparable, the nations who rise up against him and his people, *cf.*, Ps 2, are less than dust; they are in fact nothing. Paul has shown us in Rom 11:34 and 1 Cor 2:16 that the version of v. 13a given above is the correct one, not that of the RSV, "who has directed the spirit of the Lord?"

In one of the Babylonian rituals for the New Year Feast, the priest describes Marduk:

> who. . . s heaven, heaps up the earth,
> who measures the waters of the sea, cultivates the fields,
> . . . . . .
> who decrees the fates of all the gods. . . .
>
> (*ANET*, 332)

The text is late, from the Seleucid period 4th-3rd c. B.C., but according to its editors it may well go back much earlier. There is of course no ordering of the deities in Israel's theology because Yahweh is one.

40:18-31. THE UNCREATED CREATOR AND THE GODS OF HUMAN HANDS

> [18]To whom then will you liken God,
> or what likeness compare with him?
> [19]The idol! a workman casts it,
> and a goldsmith overlays it with gold,

and casts for it silver chains.
[20]He who is impoverished chooses for an offering
wood that will not rot;
he seeks out a skilful craftsman
to set up an image that will not move.

[21]Have you not known? Have you not heard?
Has it not been told you from the beginning?
Have you not understood from the foundations of the earth?
[22]It is he who sits above the circle of the earth,
and its inhabitants are like grasshoppers;
who stretches out the heavens like a curtain,
and spreads them like a tent to dwell in;
[23]who brings princes to nought,
and makes the rulers of the earth as nothing.

[24]Scarcely are they planted, scarcely sown,
scarcely has their stem taken root in the earth,
when he blows upon them, and they wither,
and the tempest carries them off like stubble.
[25]To whom then will you compare me,
that I should be like him? says the Holy One.
[26]Lift up your eyes on high and see:
who created these?
He who brings out their host by number,
calling them all by name;
by the greatness of his might
and because he is strong in power
not one is missing.

[27]Why do you say, O Jacob,
and speak, O Israel,
"My way is hid from the LORD,
and my right is disregarded by my God"?
[28]Have you not known? Have you not heard?
The LORD is the everlasting God,
the Creator of the ends of the earth.
He does not faint or grow weary,
his understanding is unsearchable.

[29]He gives power to the faint,
and to him who has no might he increases strength.
[30]Even youths shall faint and be weary,
and young men shall fall exhausted;
[31]but they who wait for the LORD shall renew their strength,
they shall mount up with wings like eagles,
they shall run and not be weary,
they shall walk and not faint.

vv. 18-20. Attention is moved from God the incomparable to the images of the gods of Babylon. This is the first of several "idol passages" (40:18-20; 41:5-7; 44:9-20; 46:5-7). The view taken in this commentary is that these polemical passages are in their correct place, deliberately set there by the prophet himself, to sharpen the contrast between Yahweh and the gods of the nations. The educated Babylonians were not so naive as to think that the images carried in procession were the gods themselves, though popular religion may well have thought so. Nevertheless there were detailed instructions similar to those in vv. 19-20 for the casting of statues in the Babylonian New Year liturgy. But even to represent God was both an abomination and an absurdity for Israel. Any image of a deity must disintegrate or rot — a sign of their worthlessness.

vv. 21-24. There follows now a series of rhetorical questions. Surely the people of Israel know the story of the beginnings! Yahweh's present saving action is rooted in his first creation action. The creator is described by three successive present participles in the manner of the psalms of descriptive praise: "he who is sitting upon the dome of the earth. . . who is stretching the heavens like a veil. . . who is reducing rulers to nothing. . .," *cf.,* Ps 104(103):2-4. The earth was conceived of as a flat disc upon the primeval deep, encircled by the primeval waters or river. The rest of the waters were above the solid dome of the heavens, Gen 1:7, and the dome itself was supported by pillars which plunged down into the primeval abyss. Such was the traditional world image. The creator sits enthroned above the earth and dominates it, Ps 33(32):13-15. The lords of the earth are as nothing before him. They are like the grass of the desert and the steppes before the breath of the Lord, *cf.,* v. 7.

vv. 25-26. The speaker changes for a brief moment in v. 25, and resumes the question of v. 18. It is the Holy One, *qādôsh*, who speaks; holy — *i.e.*, separate, apart, *cf.*, Lev 19:2; Isa 6:3. This Holy One is the creator God "who drills them (the stars) like an army. . . " in the martial image of the JB; literally "he brings their hosts out in order and calls each by name," *cf.,* Isa 45:12; 51:15; Ps 147(146-147):4. Similar imagery and language occurs in the Aramaic Wisdom of Ahiqar, 6th or 5th century B.C.:

> Many are the stars of heaven, and no man knows their names.
>
> (*ANET*, 429)

Yahweh, by giving the stars their names, gives them their destiny and has dominion over them. The word *bārā'*, the technical theological word "he created," occurs for the first time in v. 26 (see Excursus 1).

The prophet moves constantly from nature to history: from the architect of the universe, vv. 12-14, 21-22, 28 to the nations, vv. 15-17, the rulers of the earth, vv. 23-24, and the faint and weary among the exiles, vv. 29-31. The universe, the world, is the area where God acts, where history unfolds. God created the world to be lived in, 42:5; 45:12, 18. This God is the Lord of the universe and the Lord of all history, and specifically of the history of Israel.

vv. 27-31. The addressees are now mentioned by name. The self-pitying exiles are roused to life. Yahweh has not forgotten; he is not the God of a moment; he is the eternal God, "from everlasting to everlasting you are God. . . a thousand years in your sight are but as yesterday when it is past, or as a watch in the night," Ps 90(89):2, 4. If the exiles take their stand on the creator God who is the Lord of history, they will rise to heights unheard of. So there is no place for despair.

Excursus 1. Creation in Second Isaiah

The word *bārā'*, create, occurs 49 times in the Hebrew Bible, 17 times in Second Isaiah, 10 times in the priestly writing in Genesis, 3 times in Isa 56-66, 4 times in the psalms, and elsewhere. The uses are almost all late pre-exilic, exilic and post-exilic. Most exegetes take it as certain that *bārā'* is a late word and was first introduced into the Old Testament as a theological idea in the exilic period. But the biblical writers of both the Old and New Testaments were receivers and transmitters of tradition as well as contributors, and so it is very unlikely that Second Isaiah was introducing an entirely new word and idea. There was a long tradition attributing creation to the gods in Mesopotamian literature. In Israel, among her neighbours and beyond, among those groups so often called "primitive," there were separate traditions of the creation of the world and of the creation of man. The two themes are for the most part independent of each other. Some examples of the creation of the world in the psalms are: 19(18):1-2; 90(89):2; 93(92):1; 102(101):25-27; 104(103); 115(113B):15; 121(120):2; 134(133):3; of the creation of humankind: 22(21):9-10; 94(93):9; 100(99):3; 138(137):8; 139(138):13-15; in some psalms the two themes are brought together: 33(32):6-9 & 15; 89(88):9-12 & 47; 95(94):4-5 & 6. These are old traditions which have had a long history before becoming embedded in the liturgical life of Israel.

There are several characteristics of the use of *bārā'* in the Old Testament: a) God is always the subject of the verb, and specifically the God of Israel and no other; the verb says nothing about the way in which creation took place; b) there is never any mention of matter out of which God created, either as object of the verb or with a preposition: *i.e.,* it is never said that "God created this from (out of) that"; c) there are various objects of *bārā'*: i) the heavens and the earth, i.e.

the cosmos, Gen 1:1; 2:4; Isa 42:5; 45:18; ii) humankind, Gen 1:27; 5:1; 6:7; Isa 43:7; 45:12; Ezek 28:13, 15; iii) the people of Israel, Isa 43:1, 15; Ps 102(101):18 ("a created people" Hebr.); iv) something wonderful or new: Isa 48:6f; 65:17.

The verb itself does not mean "creation out of nothing," but is saying in its own thought pattern and imagery what other philosophies mean by it: God is supreme, with full dominion, free and not bound to anything. Our idea of "nothing" is a later notion stemming from Greek philosophy. It appears in Hebrew literature only after Hebrew thought had been in contact with Greek thought for a considerable time. In the second book of the Maccabees, composed in the Jewish diaspora in the 2nd century B.C., the mother of the seven brothers and martyrs addresses her youngest son: "...look at the heaven and the earth and see everything that is in them, and recognize that God did not make them out of things that existed," 2 Macc 7:28. And the book of the Wisdom of Solomon, written in the same place about 50 B.C., addresses God as wisdom: "For thy all-powerful hand, which created the world out of formless matter...," Wis 11:17. For the people of the ancient Near East, "before creation" was the opposite of the order which they experience in the universe, hence "chaos"; and chaos is expressed by darkness, wind and the clashing of the primeval waters. By creating, God draws cosmos, order, out of chaos.

In Second Isaiah the creator God is the redeemer and the lord of history. He alone can redeem and restore Israel because he along exists from the beginning and directs the history of the world. Yahweh acts with equal and absolute authority in nature and in history. Second Isaiah is an innovator in creation theology in that he unites and constantly underscores God in act as creator and redeemer. Creation for him is the beginning of sacred history, the beginning of God's acting outside himself; and history is a continuation of this creative power.

Not only has the religious idea of creation a long history, but also, it seems, has the word itself. The tablets recently discovered at Ebla, c. 2200 B.C., reveal the following place names: *é-ba-ri-um*^{ki} = temple of the creator, *ba-ra-gú*^{ki} = the voice has created, *gú-ba-ri-um*^{ki} = the voice is the creator. In each case *bārā'*, create, is a constitutive part of the word. There are scholars who consider the language of Ebla, despite its difficulties, a north-west semitic language and related to the Canaanite group to which Hebrew belongs. The idea of creation and the word *bārā'*, create, are not late innovations in Israel, but have a long history in the world of the ancient Near East.

The following are the passages in Second Isaiah where *bārā'* occurs: 40:26, 28; 41:20; 42:5; 43:1, 7, 15; 45:7 (twice), 8, 12, 18 (twice); 48:7; 54:16 (twice).

41:1-5.
WHO ROUSED CYRUS? I AM HE!

41 Be silent for me you coastlands and peoples—
let them take courage and strength.
Let them approach then speak, let us come together for judgment.
[2]Who has roused up a saviour from the east and calls him onward?
Who subdues nations and tramples kings before him?
Who makes them like dust with his sword, scatters them like dust with his bow?
[3]He pursues them, passes on safely, treads not the road with his feet.
[4]Who has done this, wrought it? He who calls the generations from the beginning —
I, Yahweh, am the first, yes, with the last! I am He!

[5]The coastlands see and are afraid; let them approach
and come!

(translation by the author)

This is the first of a series of trial speeches or disputations: 41:1-5, 21-29; 43:8-15; 44:6-8; 45:20-25. They should be read together to experience their cumulative effect. Local disputes or civil cases were held "at the city gate" where the elders sat in judgment and the people were passing by. Yahweh, the God of Israel, now summons the nations to witness two opposed claims. Who leads Cyrus (not mentioned by name here, but in 44:28; 45:1) to victory so that Israel may return home in a second exodus? Not the gods of Babylon but the Lord of history. Yahweh is the subject of v. 2a-b, Cyrus of vv. 2c-3, "he makes them. . . . he pursues them. . . ." The word translated by "saviour" in v. 2 is *sedeq-sedaqah* (both forms have the same meaning) and is very important in Second Isaiah, in Isa 56-66 and the psalms. It is often rendered by "justice," "righteousness," and at times by "victory" or "integrity" (often in JB). These versions either introduce overtones which over-interpret the text or miss the salvific impact of the word which is found almost invariably in the context of God's saving action in Isaiah and the Psalter, (see Excursus 3. *Sedeq-sedaqah*). Here it is an abstract noun, "saving action," used for the concrete, "saviour," a common device in Canaanite and Hebrew poetry. It is God ever in act who effects this; the Creator God who was there at the beginning and who will always be there, as rings out characteristically of Second Isaiah in v. 4, "I am he," *cf.*, 43:10, 13; 46:4; 48:12. Yahweh alone is God. This self-assertion or self-presentation formula is also found in Mesopotamian documents.

41:6-7.
THE IDOLS OF BABYLON

[6]Every one helps his neighbor,
and says to his brother, "Take courage!"

[7]The craftsman encourages the goldsmith,
and he who smooths with the hammer him who strikes the anvil,
saying of the soldering, "It is good";
and they fasten it with nails so that it cannot be moved.

This passage on the idols or gods of Babylon should be read with 40:19-20 and 44:9-20. The images of the deities were drawn on carts in the Babylon New Year procession. But Israel's God is beyond plastic image and comparison. The prophet describes the process of constructing the idols of Babylon. They are the work of human hands. What can they effect? In each case the idols are set in contrast to Yahweh: "to whom then will you like God?. . . ," 40:18; "I am He," 41:4; "is there a God besides me?" 44:8. These passages are often described as polemical insertions and crude caricatures which misrepresent the Babylonians' understanding of their divinities. Polemical they certainly are and there is something of the caricature. But amid the rhetoric and ridicule let us not forget that the prophet experienced Babylonian religion and was as capable as modern critics of understanding the symbolic realism of the idols. But his God could not have a beginning such as represented by the manufacture of idols.

41:8-16.
ASSURANCE OF SALVATION

(i)
[8]But you, Israel, my servant, Jacob whom I have chosen,
the offspring of Abraham, my friend;
[9]you whom I took from the ends of the earth,
and called from its farthest corners,
saying to you, "You are my servant,
I have chosen you and not cast you off";
[10]fear not, for I am with you,
be not dismayed, for I am your God;

I will strengthen you, I will help you,
I will uphold you with my victorious (saving) right hand.
[11]Behold, all who are incensed against you
shall be put to shame and confounded;
those who strive against you shall be as nothing and perish.

[12]You shall seek those who content with you,
but you shall not find them;
those who war against you shall be as nothing at all.
[13]For I, the Lord your God, hold your right hand;
it is I who say to you, "Fear not, I will help you."

(ii)
[14]Do not fear Jacob you worm, Israel you louse,
It is I who help you, oracle of Yahweh;
Yes, I your redeemer, the Holy One of Israel.
[15]Behold, I will make you a threshing sledge,
new, sharp and having teeth;
you shall thresh the mountains and crush them,
and you shall make the hills like chaff
[16]You shall winnow them and the wind shall carry them away,
and the tempest shall scatter them.
But you, you shall rejoice in Yahweh,
you shall glory in the Holy One of Israel.

(translation of vv. 14 & 16b by author).

This is the first of a group of oracles of assurance of salvation: 41:8-13, 14-16; 43:1-4, 5-7; 44:1-5. There are other oracles which proclaim salvation: 41:17-20; 42:14-17; 43:16-21; 46:1-13; 48:1-11, 12-17. Second Isaiah uses this traditional form, be its origin the consultation of a priest in a liturgical setting or the consultation of a prophet, to convey his central message. Throughout both oracles, vv. 8-13 and 14-16, it is "I," Yahweh, who acts. The first person pronoun occurs five times, twice in vv. 10 and 13, once in v. 14, and many of the verbs are in the first person. God is giving his assurance to Israel that she will continue to exist and that she is always the object of his care. Despite what the exiles may think, he has not abandoned them. They must not hand themselves over to images made by human hands.

Israel is the "religious" name of the people with all the echoes of election and destiny. Jacob is used here in the same sense. He was given the name Israel after his all-night struggle with the being at the Jabbok stream, and with it a new destiny; he became a new man, Gen 32:22-32. And Israel is being re-created as a new people.

Israel is "my servant." The word servant in the Bible moves between the meanings "belonging to" and "subordination." The former predominates in "my servant." Abraham is "my servant," Gen 26:24; so is Moses, Num 12:7; David, 2 Sam 3:18; 7:5; Ps 89(88):3, 20; and the prophets, Amos 3:7. "My servant" is Israel throughout Second Isaiah: 41:8, 9; 42:19; 43:10; 44:1, 2, 21; 45:4. And it will be argued in the commentary that "my servant" is Israel in her various aspects in what are called the Servant Songs, 42:1; 49:3; 52:13; 53:11, even though the name Israel is mentioned only once, 49:3 (see Excursus 2. The Problem of the Servant Songs). The context of vv. 8-10 is that of Abraham "my friend," and of choice and election, vv. 8-9. In fidelity to this election Yahweh will support his people "by my saving right hand," v. 10. It is simply because "I" am your God, vv. 10, 13, because "I" have chosen you, 41:8; 43:10, 20; 44:1f; 45:4, that Israel's enemies cannot prevail and that there is no need for fear. Verse 13 resumes the words of v. 10 and closes the first oracle.

Israel is only a squirming earthy creature, but it is "I" who is there with her. The "Holy One of Israel" and "redeemer" are important terms in Second Isaiah's message. The Holy One of Israel occurs 13 times, 41:14, 16, 20; 43:3, 14, 15; 45:11; 47:4; 48:17; 49:7 (twice); 54:5; 55:5. The term is often in combination with redeemer and saviour, with "he who has chosen you and he who glorifies you." It derives from Isaiah of the 8th century, *cf.*, Isa 1:4; 6:3. The "redeemer" was the one who in Israelite law came to the aid of a kinsman in trouble. Yahweh's relationship to Israel was a family one.

Three of the leading theological motifs of Second Isaiah have now been introduced — creation, history, redemption.

In the metaphor of the threshing floor Yahweh as Israel's helper, v. 15, will crush all opposition through her. In 40:4 the mountains and the hills stood in the way of the return; here they are probably the enemy seen as obstacles in her path. The final proclamation in v. 16b comes directly from the Psalter, with a change from first to second person, where the person in distress praises the wonderful acts of God.

41:17-20.
THE DESERT SPRINGS TO LIFE

[17]When the poor and needy seek water,
and there is none,
and their tongue is parched with thirst,
I the LORD will answer them,
I the God of Israel will not forsake them.
[18]I will open rivers on the bare heights,
and fountains in the midst of the valleys;
I will make the wilderness a pool of water,
and the dry land springs of water.
[19]I will put in the wilderness the cedar,
the acacia, the myrtle, and the olive;
I will set in the desert the cypress,
the plane and the pine together;
[20]that men may see and know,
may consider and understand together,
that the hand of the LORD has done this,
the Holy One of Israel has created it.

The poor and the needy are those who often stand in expectation before God in the psalms of individual and community lament. The picture here is that of the curse of the Middle East — drought, barrenness, cattle dying of thirst, *cf.,* Jer 14:2-6. But again Yahweh, "I", proclaims. The people lament, Yahweh answers. He has always heard them in the past; he will hear them again. "I" will make a way through the desert as I did before; as long as "I" am at work, no obstacle, desert, mountain or valley is insurmountable. He will do all this so that they, Israel and people beyond, may witness and experience (not just "see and know," not mere observing with a notional assent) that the one God is at work. The Holy One of Israel created, *bārā'*, this; it is something that he alone can do. "Events never happen independently of him: literally, he creates them, Isa 48:6ff," as Mgr. Charles Moeller has put it so well.

41:21-29.
YAHWEH AND "THE GODS" IN HISTORY

[21]Set forth your case, says the Lord,
bring your proofs, says the King of Jacob.
[22]Let them bring them, and tell us what is to happen.
Tell us the former things, what they are, that we may consider them,
That we may know their outcome.
[23]Tell us what is to come hereafter,
that we may know that you are gods;
do good or do harm,
that we may be dismayed and terrified.
[24]Behold, you are nothing, and your work is naught;
an abomination is he who chooses you.

[25]I stirred up one from the north, and he has come,
from the rising of the sun, and he shall call on my name;
he shall trample on rulers as on mortar,
as the potter treads clay.
[26]Who has declared it from the beginning, that he might know,
and beforetime, that we might say, "He is right"?
There was none who declared it, none who proclaimed,
none who heard your words.
[27]I first have declared it to Zion,
and I give to Jerusalem a herald of good tidings.
[28]But when I look there is no one;

among these there is no counsellor who, when I ask,
gives an answer.
[29]Behold, they are all a delusion; their works are nothing;
their molten images are empty wind.

The second trial speech falls into two parts: in vv. 21-24 Yahweh summons the gods of Babylon to state their case so as to justify their claims to be effective deities. But they can say nothing because they have done nothing; in vv. 25-29 Yahweh tells what he has proclaimed and done. He declares their claims to be non-existent. The one God confronts a plurality of gods; they have effected nothing: "your work is naught" v. 24, "their works are nothing" v. 29, *cf.*, 45:18-19. This is no abstract discussion on monotheism and polytheism, but rather a question of action in history. Three times in vv. 22-23 the gods of Babylon are called to "tell us" — tell us what happens in history in general, v. 22a, what has happened in the past, v. 22b, what is to happen in the future, v. 23a; then we will experience, v. 22b, and really know, v. 23a, that they are gods. They can give no interpretation of history as can the God of Israel when he interprets Israel's history. "Do good or do harm," *i.e.*, do anything at all to make us stand in awe — but it is all futile.

Yahweh now tells how he is the master and director of history. Taking his stand in Zion and Jerusalem (v. 27), he sees Cyrus in the north where he has moved from the east. Cyrus conquered the Median empire in 550 B.C. and moved westwards to conquer the empire of Croesus in 547 B.C. The verse which says that Cyrus "shall call on my name" raises difficulties. It has been suggested that Second Isaiah himself or a pious scribe thought that Cyrus had or would become a worshipper of Yahweh. In 45:4 Yahweh says of Cyrus: "I call you by your name. . . though you do not know me." The first Isaiah scroll from the Dead Sea reads: "and he called him by his name." The one whom Yahweh has now stirred up is, unknown to the gods of Babylon, a saviour of Israel. Yahweh alone knows this from the beginning and directs the course to its goal, the return of the exiles. The exiles had virtually given up hope, but he has seen their distress and answered their prayers. Yahweh has proclaimed and fulfilled; throughout the 8th and 7th centuries he proclaimed doom through the prophets and brought it about. The gods of Babylon can predict what they will, but they cannot effect it. They neither understand nor control history, therefore what they do is futile. Their counsel at law can say nothing!

42:1-4.
THE FIRST SERVANT SONG

42 Here is my servant whom I uphold,
my chosen one in whom is my joy;
I put my spirit upon him,
he will reveal my law to the nations;
[2]He will not cry out nor raise his voice,
nor make it heard in the street.
[3]A bruised reed he will not break,
and faintly burning flax he will not put out;
for truth's sake he will reveal my law.
[4]He will not faint, he will not be broken,
while he is setting up my law on earth,
and the coastlands will wait for his teaching.

(translation by author)

This is the first of four passages generally known as the servant songs (42:1-4; 49:1-6; 50:4-9; 52:13 - 53:12). The view taken in this commentary is that they are the work of Second Isaiah and are an integral part of chaps. 40-55 from the beginning, that they do not come from another hand, even of a disciple, and that they were not inserted later into the text (see Excursus 2. The Problem of the Servant Songs). It is maintained further that the servant is Israel, addressed or speaking or described under the figure of an individual. "The servant of the songs is thought of as an individual. . . . but he symbolized allegorically a community, namely Israel. . . . " (Johannes Lindblom). The destiny of captive Israel is spelled out in 42:1-4 and elaborated in vv. 5-9.

The language of 42:1 is very like that of 41:8-10:

41:8-10	42:1
[8]Israel my servant	[1]my servant
whom I have chosen	my chosen one
offspring of Abraham my friend	in whom is my joy
[9]you are my servant,	
I have chosen you	
[10]I will strengthen you	I put my spirit upon him
I will help you	
I will uphold you	my servant whom I uphold

The servant "will reveal my law to the nations." The word translated "law," *mishpat*, occurs three times in 42:1-4. It is rendered "justice" by RSV, NEB, NAB, New International Bible, Good News Bible, and "true justice" by JB. Other renderings are judgment, (legal) decision or sentence, true religion. Some authors understand *mishpat* out of the legal process of the previous chapter, 41:1ff; the gods of the Babylonians have been declared to be nothing; there is one God only, Yahweh. This is the judgment, *mishpat*, that is to be made known to the nations.

The translation "my law" proceeds from the parallelism between *mishpat* and *tôrāh* in v. 4. *Tôrāh* means teaching or instruction. It is God's "way," Ps 119(118):30. Jeremiah speaks of those who "do not know the way of the Lord, the law (*mishpat*) of their God," Jer 5:4. Second Isaiah summons the people to listen, "for instruction (*tôrāh*) will go forth from me, and my law (*mishpat*) for a light to the peoples," 51:4. The Servant himself is to be a light to the nations, Isa 42:6; 49:6. Habakkuk notes that "instruction (*tôrāh*) is slacked, and my law (*mishpat*) never goes forth," 1:4. The Servant will establish "my law" on earth, *i.e.* "the sum-total of divine requirements" (J. Lindblom), all that is required for an ordered life before Yahweh. He will not behave like a victorious king with proclamation in the market-place and the crushing of opposition, but quietly, respecting the faint glimmerings of hope that may still remain, vv. 2-3. Israel will not conquer by the sword, but as a living example of obedience to God's law will bring light to the world.

42:5-9.
THE SERVANT FURTHER....

[5]Thus says God, the Lord,
who created the heavens and stretched them out,
who spread forth the earth and what comes from it,
who gives breath to the people upon it
and spirit to those who walk in it:
[6]"I am the Lord, I have called you in righteousness,
I have taken you by the hand and kept you;
I have given you as a covenant to the people, a
light to the nations,
[7]to open the eyes that are blind,
to bring out the prisoners from the dungeon,
from the prison those who sit in darkness.
[8]I am the Lord, that is my name;
my glory I give to no other,
nor my praise to graven images.
[9]Behold, the former things have come to pass,
and new things I now declare;
before they spring forth, I tell you of them."

The passage is introduced by the usual oracle formula, v. 5, and continues with a series of present participles in the manner of a hymn or psalm of descriptive praise, *cf.*, Ps 104(103):1-5. The creator God speaks, calls in his saving purpose, and assigns a role, vv. 6-7; the call is set between the repeated assertion "I Yahweh," vv. 6a and 8a, combining the 1st person pronoun and the proper name. The creator is the Lord of history; in history he creates anew, v. 9. The passage presumes the first servant song, in which the servant's destiny is to bring God's law to the nations, and elaborates it. The servant we have identified as Israel addressed under the figure of a person. The "you" of v. 6 is in the singular, of v. 9 in the plural, where Israel is again the addressee, the announcement being made to the exiles.

The language of v. 6, "I called," "I took," is similar to that of 41:9. God calls Israel *b^{e}sedeq*, in his saving purpose, just as he rouses Cyrus *b^{e}sedeq* in 45:13. The chosen one is to be literally "a covenant of people" and "a light of nations." The word "people" refers to humankind in general, as does the same word in v. 5. But what of covenant, *berît*? Following the very convincing work of E. Kutsch we understand covenant as either the obligation which the subject making or imposing the *berît* takes upon himself, or the obligation he imposes on the other. From this there developes the idea of a mutual *berît* and, consequently, the secondary and rather rare use of the word in the more popular sense of covenant. "It is of particular theological significance that the Old Testament.... knows nothing of a mutual *berît* with complementary obligations agreed on by God and man" (E. Kutsch).

Covenant *berît* is understood here in the sense of assurance (in Gen 15:7-21, non-P, a solemn assurance by God is enacted ritually; in Gen 17, P, God himself gives a solemn assurance; in each case it is a *berît*); there are also the overtones of life, well-being, peace, which the biblical writers include under *shālôm* (K. Elliger), *cf.,* Isa 32:15-17. Israel then is to be an "assurance (pledge) to the people"; she is also to be a "light of nations"; the second phrase is parallel to the first and forms a whole with it, saying virtually the same thing. The light is not that of revelation so much as of liberation. The line may be rendered: "I will make you a pledge to the people(s), I will put you a light to the nations, opening the eyes that are blind. . . . " Yahweh acts through his instrument, freeing the nations from their slavery to false gods and beliefs. He, the true God, affirms himself and yields his glory and honour to none, v. 8.

The former things that have come to pass probably concern the fate of the people in days past or the rise of Cyrus. The new things are concerned with the destiny of Israel which, as God's chosen one, has a new function in history. It is this that he wants the exiles to hear.

42:10-17.
A NEW SONG —
YAHWEH WILL LEAD THE EXILES HOME

(i) vv. 10-13.

> [10]Sing to the Lord a new song,
> his praise from the end of the earth!
> Let the sea roar and all that fills it,
> the coastlands and their inhabitants.
> [11]Let the desert and its cities lift up their voice,
> the villages that Kedar inhabits;
> let the inhabitants of Sela sing for joy,
> let them shout from the top of the mountains.
> [12]Let them give glory to the Lord,
> and declare his praise in the coastlands.
> [13]The Lord goes forth like a mighty man,
> like a man of war he stirs up his fury;
> he cries out, he shouts aloud,
> he shows himself mighty against his foes.

In v. 9 of the previous passage Yahweh declares new things. Here the exiles, pagans and the whole earth are summoned to respond to Yahweh's "new creation" with a new song. The hymn, vv. 10-13, is a genuine psalm; there is not a phrase that does not appear in the Psalter; the opening words are those of Pss 96(95); 98(97); and new song is sung in Pss 33(32):3; 40(39):3; 144(143):9. R. N. Whybray has pointed out that there are three elements here: i) a summons to praise, vv. 10-12, ii) a statement about Yahweh, v. 13, iii) a speech by Yahweh. The first two follow the pattern of a hymn of praise; the third does not. Hence the view of many that we have in vv. 10-17 two separate units.

God has made his decision to free the people, a decision that is firm and present to him, but for the people to be effective only in the future. Yet all are to acknowledge this act now — exiles (the addressees), the desert tribes (Kedar: in the Syro-Arabian desert; Sela — rock: probably the rose-red city of Petra in southern Jordan), the coastlands.

This hymn has been described as "eschatological." In the context of Second Isaiah this does not refer to the two eras characteristic of intertestamental apocalyptic. It means the future, certainly, but it is a future very much of this world where life and land will approach the ideal. The Lord, Yahweh, who is to do this, who is the creator acting in history, is described in the ancient traditional imagery of the warrior, Ex 15:3; Deut 4:17; Zeph 3:17; Pss 24(23):8; 78(77):65. He stirs up his fury, *qin'ah*, that is his zeal or jealousy, the term used of the jealous God whose glory and praise may be given to no other, Ex 20:5; Deut 5:9.

(ii) vv. 14-17.

[14]For a long time I have held my peace,
I have kept still and restrained myself;
now I will cry out like a woman in travail,
I will gasp and pant.
[15]I will lay waste mountains and hills,
and dry up all their herbage
I will turn the rivers into islands,
and dry up the pools.
[16]And I will lead the blind
in a way that they know not,
in paths that they have not known I will guide them.
I will turn the darkness before them into light,
the rough places into level ground.
These are the things I will do,
and I will not forsake them.
[17]They shall be turned back and utterly put to shame,
who trust in graven images,
who say to molten images, "You are our gods."

Yahweh admits his inaction — during the exile and long before. Now he will burst into action — there will be a new birth. The language of vv. 15-16 is very like that of 41:18-20. Though in reverse — vv. 15-16 will dry up rivers and land, 41:18-20 will make the wilderness into springs of water —both passages are saying the same thing: Yahweh will step into history and lead his people back. The blind are the exiles who will see the light (see other references to "the blind" in 42:7; 42:19). Yahweh does not accuse his people of worshipping idols; he is content to state how futile are those who trust in graven images.

42:18 — 43:7

BLIND ISRAEL — FEAR NOT

[18]Hear, you deaf; and look, you blind, that you may see!
[19]Who is blind but my servant
or deaf as my messenger whom I send?
Who is blind as the servant of the Lord?
or blind as the servant of the Lord?
[20]He sees many things, but does not observe them;
his ears are open, but he does not hear.
[21]The Lord was pleased, for his righteousness' sake,
to magnify his law and make it glorious.
[22]But this is a people robbed and plundered,
they are all of them trapped in holes and hidden in prisons;
they have become a prey with none to rescue,
a spoil with none to say, "Restore!"
[23]Who among you will give ear to this,
will attend and listen for the time to come?
[24]Who gave Jacob up to the spoiler,
and Israel to the robbers?
Was it not the Lord, against whom we have sinned,
in whose ways they would not walk,
and whose law they would not obey?
[25]So he poured upon him the heat of his anger

and the might of battle;
it set him on fire round about, but he did not understand;
it burned him, but he did not take it to heart.

43:1-7

43 But now thus says the Lord,
he who created you, O Jacob,
he who formed you, O Israel:
"Fear not, for I have redeemed you;
I have called you by name, you are mine.
[2]When you pass through the waters I will be with you;
and through the rivers, they shall not overwhelm you;
when you walk through fire you shall not be burned,
and the flame shall not consume you.
[3]For I am the Lord your God,
the Holy One of Israel, your Saviour.
I give Egypt as your ransom,
Ethiopia and Seba in exchange for you.
[4]Because you are precious in my eyes
and honoured and I love you,
I give men in return for you,
peoples in exchange for your life.
[5]Fear not, for I am with you;
I will bring your offspring from the east,
and from the west I will gather you;
[6]I will say to the north, Give up,
and to the south, Do not withhold;
bring my sons from afar
and my daughters from the end of the earth,
[7]everyone who is called by my name,
whom I created for my glory,
whom I formed and made."

The first part of this section, 42:18-25, is made difficult by the change in person, "(you) see many things, yet you (sing.) do not observe them; (he) opens (his) ears yet he does not hear," v. 20, and "we have sinned against him, but they will not walk in his ways nor listen to his teaching," v. 24. There is also a series of infinitives in vv. 20 and 22, and four questions each beginning with "who" vv. 19a, 19b, 23, 24. The wording of v. 22 is typical of the 1st person plural lament but is in the 3rd person, while v. 21 with its reference to God's saving purpose and law seems to interrupt the flow from v. 20 to v. 22. Hence C. R. North remarks that the passage "reads more like a poet's notes than a finished poem." Many commentators, therefore, regard it as a poem which has been expanded by later additions and interpretations; these additions would be vv. 19b, 21, 24b.

But what sort of a poem is it? what is its form? The most helpful suggestion is that of Claus Westermann who understands it as a reply by Yahweh to a community lament in which he is accused of being blind and deaf to the fate of his people (*cf.*, 40:27). Yahweh replies with a series of questions which determine the meaning: "who is blind if not my servant...?" vv. 19a and 19b; "who among you will give ear to this...?" v. 23; "who has handed Jacob over to the spoiler...?" v. 24. Despite the difficulties, the meaning is clear enough: it is not Yahweh who is blind and deaf, but "my servant," "my messenger," "my covenanted one" — Israel. Israel is too blind and too deaf to see and realize that it is through her own fault that she is in ruins and in exile, and that it is Yahweh, not the power of Babylon, who has determined her fate.

The theme of blindness, though in different senses, has already been sounded, 42:7, 16, and will be sounded again, 43:8. The reference to the glorification of the law in v. 21 recalls Ps 119(118). It is God's pleasure to extol and glorify his law because of his saving purpose, *sedeq* v. 21 (here, almost the equivalent of *hesed*, his steadfast love). The imagery of v. 22 should not be pushed to the letter; it is typical of a community lament. Finally, the people of Israel have experienced the anger of God, v. 25, but are too obtuse to understand what is going on; they are like one who stands in the midst of a fire, is scorched, and cannot notice it.

"But now Yahweh has spoken thus....," 43:1. The blind are now addressed in two oracles of salvation and assurance, "Do not be afraid, for I have redeemed you," v. 1; "Do not be afraid, for I am with you," v. 5. It is here that we have the heart of the message of Second Isaiah; it is in sharp contrast to what has immediately preceded. By means of a literary inclusion, the two oracles are framed within creation — "your creator, Jacob, your fashioner, Israel," v. 1; and "I have created, I have fashioned, I have made you," v. 7. The word create, *bārā'*, is characteristic of the first creation account (Gen 1:1 - 2:4a), fashion, *yasar*, of the second (Gen 2:4b-25), while "make" is common to both. It is the creator of Israel and the creator of the world who is the redeemer and the maker of history. An important theme of these verses is "I. . . . you": "I have called you by your name, you are mine," v. 1; ". . . . I love you," v. 4; "I am with you," v. 5; "everyone who is called by my name, whom I created . . . ," v. 7.

The real meaning of election is concentrated in these oracles: "I created. . . . I fashioned. . . . I redeemed. . . . I called," v. 1 (*cf.*, 40:12-26, 28; 42:5), and "you are precious in my eyes, you are of worth, and I love you," v. 4. Abraham, the person in whom Israel was chosen, is "Abraham whom I love," 41:8. Yahweh's protecting hand will be there always, v. 2, and this is expressed in the language of the psalms, Pss 66(65):2; 91(90):7-13, and in that continuous thread, "fear not," which appears again, 43:1, 5, see 40:9; 41:10, 13; 44:2, 54:4. Yahweh's liberating action in Israel's favour will extend to Egypt, upper Egypt and the lower Sudan, v. 5, as he gathers his own almost literally from the four quarters of the earth to be one people, v. 6. Not only is Israel as a people called by his name, *i.e.,* the elect, but also every individual, v. 7. Yahweh created Israel once, now he creates, fashions, makes her again "for my glory," so that all, Israel and non-Israel, will acknowledge him as the lord of history. And with this new creation Israel has a new destiny, to be Yahweh's peaceful light to the nations.

Second Isaiah's message is spoken into the immediate situation of the 540's B.C. It is meant for that. But the assurance, "I am with you," and the claim that his action is "to my glory," *i.e.,* in order that people may acknowledge me for what I am, holds for all time.

43:8-13.
DISPUTE — GOD OR GODS?

[8]Bring forth the people who are blind, yet have eyes,
who are deaf, yet have ears!
[9]Let all the nations gather together,
and let the peoples assemble.
Who among them can declare this,
and show us the former things?
Let them bring their witnesses to justify them,
and let them hear and say, It is true.
[10]"You are my witnesses," says the Lord,
"and my servant whom I have chosen,
that you may know and believe me
and understand that I am He.
Before me no god was formed,
nor shall there be any after me.
[11]I, I am the Lord,
and besides me there is no savior.
[12]I declared and saved and proclaimed,
when there was no strange god among you;
and you are my witnesses," says the Lord.
[13]"I am God, and also henceforth I am He;
there is none who can deliver from my hand;
I work and who can hinder it?

We have here another disputation passage. It is a confrontation at law to which blind and deaf Israel, v. 8, and the nations, v. 9, are summoned to state their case. The matter of the dispute is: God or gods? or, to put it another way, the claim to divinity by Babylon's gods and Yahweh. The case can only be decided by reference to history; who foretold what will happen and who brought it about? What is the evidence so that the court may give the verdict, "It is true?" v. 9c.

Blind though Israel is, *cf.*, 42:18-25, she can nevertheless be a witness. She has persistently failed to see and hear God in her history, but has experienced enough so that her perception is not entirely blinded. Yahweh has chosen "my servant," Israel, v. 10, and "you," the exiles, "that you may know and believe me and understand that I am he," *i.e.*, that Israel, individually and collectively, may go through an experience in history which will lead her to the conviction that there is but one, unique God. Knowledge, belief, understanding must not be thought of in the abstract or purely intellectually. Knowledge for the Israelite was above all experiential and empirical.

The first person singular of the pronoun, *'ănî*, *'ānokî*, "I," is used six times in vv. 10b-13. Second Isaiah is thereby asserting strict monotheism. Not only is Yahweh the One, he is the only One; other gods are not simply powerless, ineffective; they do not exist. "Before me no god was formed, after me there shall be none." There was no theogony, no story of the origins of the gods, in Israel, as there was in Babylon where the gods came out of the waters of chaos. That was unthinkable for Israel. It is Yahweh who is the only saviour, v. 11, the one universal God, who has chosen Israel; there was never a time when he did not exist. Verse 12a takes up and resolves the question put to the witnesses in v. 9; v. 12b is better understood in the sense, "I was no stranger in your midst," *i.e.*, Israel's history is a history with God. Yahweh plans, foretells, effects and directs; he is Yahweh always the same, yesterday, today, for ever, v. 13, *cf.*, Heb 13:8.

43:14-15.
INCOMPLETE ORACLE

[14]Thus says the Lord,
your Redeemer, the Holy One of Israel:
"For your sake I will send to Babylon
and break down all the bars,

and the shouting of the Chaldeans will be turned to
lamentations.
[15]I am the Lord, your Holy One,
the Creator of Israel, your King."

This is another, apparently incomplete, oracle. It has a typical beginning and end which heap up many of the descriptive terms which Second Isaiah regularly applies to Yahweh. The general sense is clear, that Yahweh will act against Babylon, though many commentators consider that the text of v. 14bii is corrupt beyond restoration. Westermann suggests that they may have been part of 43:1-7; but this does not help much.

Yahweh will reach out against Babylon — but to do what? He will "cause to break down" something, all of them (whatever they are), together with the Chaldeans, *i.e.,* the Babylonians (*cf.,* the parallelism in 48:14, 20); then follows, literally, "in ships their joy or boast." Writing v. 14b in chiastic parallelism we have:

and I will cause to go down (*i.e.* sink)
in ??? all of them

the Chaldeans in ships, their boast.

The unknown word is in parallelism with ships and this suggests that it means something the same. A slight emendation of the Hebrew letter *heth* to *he* gives a word for a boat which is attested in Ugaritic (a Canaanite language, a group to which Hebrew belongs) together with the same word for ship which appears in the second part of this verse. The following tentative translation is therefore proposed:

and I will sink them in their boats,
yes the Chaldeans in the ships in which they boast.

The boat may well refer to the *kuffa*, a circular transport vessel made of hide, attested on seals and bas-reliefs, and still used on the Tigris and Euphrates today.

43:16-21.
SOMETHING NEW

[16]Thus says the Lord,
who makes a way in the sea,
a path in the mighty waters,
[17]who brings forth chariot and horse,
army and warrior;
they lie down, they cannot rise,
they are extinguished, quenched like a wick:
[18]"Remember not the former things,
nor consider the things of old.
[19]Behold, I am doing a new thing;
now it springs forth, do you not perceive it?
I will make a way in the wilderness
and rivers in the desert.
[20]The wild beasts will honour me,
the jackals and the ostriches;
for I give water in the wilderness,
rivers in the desert,
to give drink to my chosen people,
[21]the people whom I formed for myself
that they might declare my praise.

This is a proclamation of salvation similar to 41:17-20 and 42:14-17. The beginning is typical of the hymn of praise, with the messenger formula followed by a succession of present participles, "who makes a way...," v. 16, "who marshals chariot and horse," v. 17. Yahweh, the Lord of history, not only leads his people out of Egypt but also controls the assembly of Pharaoh's army. The references in vv. 16-18 are clearly to the exodus. The "former things" of v. 18 are not in this case the deeds of Cyrus; they are defined further as "the things of old," *qadmoniyyot*, i.e. belonging to the ancient history of Israel. But what does Second Isaiah mean when he tells the exiles not to remember or consider the events of old? His words are not simply rhetorical, nor is he saying that the events of old are nothing in comparison with what he will do. He holds too firmly to the traditions of his people for this. He is telling the exiles not to look back mournfully into the past like people who have no hope for the future. Yahweh's saving acts are not at an end. He is doing something new, v. 19; it is happening now; don't they experience it in the continuous movement of history? Faith is not something dead; it must always be expectant and issue in hope. He who redeemed them from Egypt is always at work and is now creating anew. The language of v. 19b evokes Isa 35:8-10; 40:3-4 and 35:6-7; 41:18-19. Yahweh will now lead them through the desert once more, but through a different desert and in a different way. There were miracles before, there will be miracles again, for nothing is impossible with God, nothing beyond his competence, *cf.,* Gen 18:14; Lk 1:37. Even the wild animals will honour him as he provides for his people whom he has chosen and formed (a creation word), vv. 20b, 21a. And to what purpose? "that they might declare my praise"; to praise God is to acknowledge and to tell and re-tell his wonderful acts as history runs on. God is not leading his people into a permanent state of static bliss, but awakening them to the part they must play in making known his acts in history.

It is a poet who is describing Yahweh's saving acts; what is important is not the literal fulfilment, but the fact that Yahweh acts and restores his people.

43:22-28. SINFUL ISRAEL

[22]Yet it was not me you invoked, Jacob.
indeed not for me you wearied yourself, Israel.
[23]You did not bring me sheep for burnt offerings,
nor did you honour me with your sacrifices.
I did not make you serve with offerings,
nor weary you with frankincense,
[24]You did not buy me fragrant cane with your money,
nor did you satisfy me with the fat of your sacrifices.

But you made me serve with your sins,
you wearied me with your iniquities.

(translation by author)

[25]I, I am He
who blots out your transgressions for my own sake,
and I will not remember your sins.
[26]Put me in remembrance, let us argue together;
set forth your case, that you may be proved right.
[27]Your first father sinned,
and your mediators transgressed against me.
[28]Therefore I profaned the princes of the sanctuary,
I delivered Jacob to utter destruction
and Israel to reviling.

This complex and, at first sight, rather incoherent passage becomes readily intelligible when it is realized that the framework is that of both trial speech and disputation. Yahweh is addressing the exiles as the Israel of history, *i.e.*, as one with Israel who sinned from the beginning and continued to sin through centuries. Verses 22-24 are Yahweh's accusation against Israel — a cult which has long become formalized and empty of meaning; v. 25 is a declaration of conditional forgiveness; in v. 26 Yahweh calls on Israel to state its case, but Israel has nothing to say; vv. 27-28 sum up Yahweh's defence of his action — Israel's punishment is a direct consequence of a long history of sin.

vv. 22-23a. Israel's invocation of Yahweh and her sacrifices were self-serving and hollow, as Amos 5:21ff; Micah 6:6ff; Isa 1:10ff had experienced. Verses 23a and 24a are strictly parallel and are saying the same thing, namely how worthless and futile had been the external worship. Verses 23b and 24b are also in parallelism: in v. 23b Yahweh says that he did not make Israel serve by demands for offerings, nor weary her with demands for frankincense; in v. 24b he makes the most damning accusation: Israel has reversed the roles and has tried to reduce Yahweh to the status of a servant; she had expected her purely formal sacrifices to elicit an automatic response, turning Yahweh into an instrument of her selfishness. Israel had made the creator God and the redeemer her slave. This is consummate blasphemy.

But Yahweh, and he alone, can and does now wipe out Israel's sins because he is what he is (rather than "for my own sake"). Now come the formal court proceedings. Yahweh says in v. 26: "State your case against me, let us argue it out together; declare your charge that you may vindicate yourself." But Israel has nothing to say. Yahweh then gives the final judgment, vv. 27-28. Israel was a sinner from the beginning, and that is why Yahweh destroyed both kingdoms, north and south. The first father is most likely Jacob because Second Isaiah uses Jacob/Israel constantly as a patronymic title in chaps. 40-48. It is most improbable that there is reference to the first man in Gen 3. It is uncertain who the "mediators" are; the word is understood also as "interpreters" or "spokesman". Priests, prophets and kings were all mediators in various ways. The "princes of the sanctuary" in v. 28 could be the kings of Israel or the heads of the priestly families, 2 Chr 24:5. The latter however may not be a pre-exilic or exilic term.

44:1-8, 21-23.
SALVATION IS ASSURED

44"But how hear, O Jacob my servant,
Israel whom I have chosen!
[2]Thus says the Lord who made you,
who formed you from the womb and will help you:
Fear not, O Jacob my servant,
Jeshurun whom I have chosen.
[3]For I will pour water on the thirsty land,
and streams on the dry ground;
I will pour my Spirit upon your descendants,
and my blessing on your offspring.
[4]They shall spring up like grass amid waters,
like willows by flowing streams.

[5]This one will say, 'I am the Lord's,'
another will call himself by the name of Jacob,
and another will write on his hand 'The Lord's,'
and surname himself by the name of Israel."

[6]Thus says the Lord, the King of Israel
and his Redeemer, the Lord of hosts:
"I am the first and I am the last
besides me there is no god.
[7]Who is like me? Let him proclaim it,
let him declare and set it forth before me.
Who has announced from of old the things to come?
Let them tell us what is yet to be.
[8]Fear not, nor be afraid;
have I not told you from of old and declared it?
And you are my witnesses!
Is there a God besides me?
There is no Rock; I know not any".

[21]Remember these things, O Jacob,
and Israel, for you are my servant;
I formed you, you are my servant;
O Israel, you will not be forgotten by me.
[22]I have swept away your transgressions like a cloud,
and your sins like a mist;
return to me, for I have redeemed you.

[23]Sing, O heavens, for the Lord has done it;
shout, O depths of the earth;
break forth into singing, O mountains,
O forest, and every tree in it!
For the Lord has redeemed Jacob,
and will be glorified in Israel.

Commentators are not unanimous about the grouping of the verses in this chapter. Some read vv. 1-8 as one oracle, others consider that an oracle vv. 6-8, 21-22 (with or without v. 23) has been interrupted by the insertion of vv. 9-20, the mocking of the idols (whether from Second Isaiah or not, whether poetry or not); some take v. 23 separately as an eschatological hymn of praise like 42:10-13, which follows the structure of such hymns, or, as Claus Westermann, a hymn of praise which rounds off the section which began with 42:14. This commentary will first treat vv. 1-5 and 6-8 as two oracles, then look at vv. 21-22, and finally try to come to terms with the passage against the idols, vv. 9-20.

vv. 1-5. An oracle and assurance of salvation, *cf.*, 43:8-13. The opening words "but now" link it loosely with what has preceded, from which there may well be some carry over, especially from 43:25. Again it is "my servant," "my chosen one," who is addressed, *cf.*, 41:8; 42:1; 43:10. This oracle is introduced by the usual messenger formula in v. 2; Yahweh," who made you and formed you from the womb," will help you. Israel believed that Yahweh was continuously at work fashioning the child to be from the moment of conception, as well attested in Job 10:10-11; Ps 139(138):13ff. So too he was there forming Israel before she was ever a people. God's shaping, creating hand was there in the election of Abraham and Jacob. The vocabulary is already familiar from 43:1, 7. The elect therefore has every reason to expect Yahweh's help. The title Jeshurun in v. 2 occurs elsewhere only in Deut 32:15; 33:5, 26; it may be related to the Hebrew *yashar*, upright.

The reason why Israel is not to be afraid is not because of something that Yahweh has done in the past, as is usually the case in such oracles, but what he will do in the future, v. 3. Literally:

> I will pour water on the thirsty,
> and streams of rain on the dry land,
> I will pour my spirit on your children
> and my blessing on your posterity.

The parallelism shows clearly that the reference is not to the miracles in the desert, but to Israel in the future; Israel is the thirsty one, the dry land. "My spirit" is the life-giving spirit of Yahweh: Gen 2:7; Isa 32:15; Ps 104(103):30; and blessing means fertility and posterity, Gen 1:22, 28. The descendants of Israel shall sprout like a leafy (verdant) poplar (rather than like grass amid waters), like willows by flowing streams, an image well known in the Bible, *e.g.*, Ps 1.

There is an abrupt transition to v. 5. "This one — another — another..." are individual non-Israelites who witness Israel's extraordinary growth. As a consequence, they want to belong to Yahweh who effects such growth and so to become his people. The destiny of Israel therefore is not to bring about the mass conversion of the nations. Rather she is to be a witness who will attract individuals. In v. 5 Yahweh is in parallelism with Jacob and Israel, *i.e.*, one worships Yahweh by becoming a member of the people.

"One says I (belong) to Yahweh," l^{e}Yahweh. Archaeologists have found many jar handles from the period of the monarchy bearing the inscription *l^{e}melek* or l^{e} (proper name), "belonging to the king" or "belonging to X." The translation of v. 5b is uncertain. There is no preposition in the Hebrew, but simply "his hand," apparently the object of "he will write." Some authors think that a preposition has fallen out and that "with (by) his hand" or "on his hand" should be read. Some would see a reference to the practice of slaves in parts of the ancient world who branded or tatooed the name of their master of deity on their hand. However it is probably best to understand "his hand" as an accusative object, as we would write, "witness my hand..." (C. R. North). The new convert will take the name of Israel and profess allegiance in word and writing.

vv. 6-8. The messenger formula introduces words which resume and summarize some important ideas already stated: 1) Yahweh is the only true God because he is the Lord of history; 2) the gods of the nations can substantiate no claim to proclamation and fulfilment. Yahweh summons the gods of the nations to state their case in court, *cf.,* 41:1-5; 41:21-28; 43:8-15. Yahweh is Israel's king; in 41:21 he is Jacob's king, in 43:15 he is "your king." The redeemer title is repeated with the ancient title "lord of hosts" which, rather than referring here to Yahweh as the lord of Israel's armies, is more suggestive of his majesty. W. Eichrodt suggests that "hosts" means "the content of all that exists in heaven and earth." When used in the singular *saba'* often means "the stars," "the heavenly bodies," Gen 2:1; Isa 40:26; 45:12. Yahweh makes his claim to divinity, 7a, because he is the lord of history, 7b. The RSV translation of 7b requires some rearrangement of the Hebrew consonants. As they stand they may be rendered: "Since I fixed from eternity even future events, let them please tell us what they are to be." Eternity is not our abstract notion; it means rather from that time long ago when Yahweh began to intervene in history. Finally there is the direct address of assurance to the witness, namely Israel. Yahweh alone has proved his trustworthiness in proclamation and fulfilment: "You are my witnesses — is there a god besides me? no, I know no rock." The word rock as an epithet for Yahweh occurs 33 times in the Old Testament, mainly in Deuteronomy and the psalms; God is not *like* a rock, he *is* a rock, *e.g.*, Ps 62(61):2, 6, 7. Israel has every reason for confidence.

vv. 21-22. It is likely that these verses refer back to v. 8 whether they continue that oracle or not. "These things" would be Yahweh's constant proclamation and fulfilment; this is the reason why Israel is to return in confidence. Verse 21 resumes "my servant" and "I formed you" from 44:1-2. The forgiveness of sins in v. 22 recalls 43:25, and the simile recalls Hos 6:4; Job 30:15. The emphasis is on that which in God's sight lasts but a moment. God has taken the initiative in forgiving Israel, so there is every reason to return with confidence. Again it is God the redeemer, *cf.,* 43:1, 14; 44:6.

v. 23. This is a short, self-contained hymn of praise identical with those in the Psalter, *cf.,* Ps 117(116). C. Westermann regards it as the deliberate conclusion to the whole section 42:14-44:22; it is not just a separate piece, as it were sewn on. It may be compared with 42:10-13. Yahweh has acted in history, v. 23a, and for this reason the heavens and the ends of the earth, the mountains and the trees of the forest, are called to respond. He who acts in history, v. 23a, he who redeems, v. 23c, can make this summons to the universe near and far because he is its creator. His act of redemption is imminent and will be his crowning achievement — this is the sense of the last word of v. 23, rendered by "will be glorified."

44:9-20.
SATIRE ON THE MAKING OF IDOLS

[9]The fashioners of idols are all of them futile,
  and their objects of devotion are in vain.
 As for their witnesses, they do not see, they do not hear,
  so that they are ashamed.
[10]He who fashions a god has but cast an idol,
  and to no avail.
[11]See, all its devotees are ashamed,
  all its craftsmen but men.
 Let them assemble, all of them, let them all take their stand,
  let them be afraid and tremble together.
[12]The craftsman in iron incises,
  he works over the coals;
 with a hammer he fashions it,
  he forms it with a strong arm.
 Yes, he is hungry and has no strength,
  he drinks no water and is faint.
[13]The craftsman in wood stretches out a line,
  he sketches with a stylus.
 He forms it with a chisel,
  and with compasses he traces an outline.
 Then he shapes it in the figure of a man,
  in the beauty of a man, to set it in a temple.
[14]Yes, he cuts down cedars, he takes a cypress and an oak,
  he chooses among the trees of the forest,
  he plants a laurel and the rain makes it grow.
[15]It becomes a thing for man to burn;
  he takes some of it to warm himself.
 Yes, he makes a fire with it and bakes bread.
 Indeed he makes a god and worships it,

he makes an image and falls before it.
[16]Half of it he burns in the fire,
with half of it he roasts meat and eats the roast and is satisfied.
Now he warms himself and says:
Ah! I am warm, I feel the fire.
[17]The rest of it he makes into a god,
into an image before which men fall and worship.
And he prays to it and says:
Save me, for you are my god.
[18]They do not know, and they do not perceive,
for their eyes are smeared so they do not see,
their senses, so they do not understand.
[19]They do not lay it to heart,
they have not the knowledge nor the perception to say:
"Half of it I burnt in the fire, I even baked bread upon its coals,
I roasted meat and ate it.
The rest I made into an abomination,
before a block of wood I fall."
[20]A herder of ashes — a deluded mind has led him astray;
no, it cannot save his life,
nor can he say, "Have I not a lie in my right hand."

(translation by author)

The majority of scholars consider this passage to be non-Isaian and a later insertion by a lesser poet which breaks the continuity between vv. 6-8 and 21-22. It is very often treated as prose. However the new edition of the Hebrew Bible from Stuttgart (1966-76) prints the passage in verse form, and with justification, and more scholars now regard this "Satire on the Making of Idols" (James Muilenburg) as the work of Second Isaiah. This commentary follows the latter opinion, namely that it is both verse and from Second Isaiah. Further, a good case can be made for considering vv. 9-20 as part of a larger unit, vv. 6-22.

This mocking-song or satire should be read with 40:19f; 41:6f; 42:17; 45:6f; 46:1f; 5ff.

In v. 8b Yahweh asks, "Is there a God besides me?" The prophet now turns to the images of the gods in Babylon. He is not presenting a treatise on idolatry, but preaching a popular satire on the futility of the idol makers. He has obviously seen them at their craft.

The idols or images of Babylon are *tohû*, v. 9, that which was there before God turned chaos into cosmos, the opposite of meaningful and ordered existence; the idols are utter futility. Verse 10 is not a question but should read, "he who fashions a god, has but cast it an idol and to no avail." The words in v. 11b are those used to summon adversaries to court, though no court scene follows.

The prophet now describes the manufacture of idols. The structure of vv. 12-20, following C. Westermann, is:

[12]the work of the ironsmith
[13]the work of the carpenter
[14]the procuring of material
[15f] the use made of it; for cooking and for making a god
[17]worship offered to the wood
[18]a marginal note on the absurdity of such an act
[19]he does not know what he does!
[20]the conclusion of the whole oracle; the makers of idols are to be put to shame.

"The section is a masterpiece of satirical writing" (Westermann). The focus is entirely on the men at work. How stupid they are — they cannot see that the wood which they use to make a fire, to cook their food, to carve an idol is all one and the same — perishable. All they are left with in the end is a heap of ashes.

Virtually all commentators follow the judgment of Bernhard Duhm, 1892, on the idol satire:

> There is no need to prove that the author, as is generally the case in later Jewish polemics, touches only the external side of the worship of images and not the real meaning; rather it is proof of how far removed were the Jews

> from their pagan fellows and how haughtily they disdained them, for what they [the pagans] did was to transfer all sorts of magical powers and qualities from the Numen that inhabited the image to the image itself; but even the simplest [Jewish] worshipper no more confuses image and Numen than does the Jew Elijah with his mantle.

James Muilenburg writes: "The prophet seems nowhere to reveal any true understanding of the pagan mind on this subject." And so the chorus continues. Second Isaiah's attitude is continued in the deutero-canonical Book of Wisdom from Alexandria, written about 50 B.C., chaps. 13-14, especially 13:11-13. And the Roman poet Horace wrote in his Satires, I, viii, 1ff.: "Once I was a fig-tree trunk, a useless log, when the craftsman, hesitant whether to make a bench or a Priapus (god of the garden), chose that I be a god."

It is important not to read later distinctions and refinements back into Second Isaiah. It is equally important to remember the literary form and tone with its bitter irony and exaggerations. Just as important too is the distinction between official religion and popular piety and its manifestations. One only has to think of the quasi-magical veneration of images today in some parts of the Catholic Church as contrasted with the official teaching about them. And Second Isaiah was a little closer to actual popular Babylonian religion than we are. Let us give him the credit for first-hand personal experience and let us not write off his satires in the light of a pseudo-superior sophistication of the 19th or 20th century, often the fruit of an overdose of Enlightenment. What was of supreme importance for him was that there was one, unique creator God and redeemer. If any of the exiles were won over by the spectacular Babylonian processions and ceremonies, then they were won over to futility.

44:24 — 45:7.
CYRUS, YAHWEH'S ANOINTED

[24]Thus says the LORD, your Redeemer,
who formed you from the womb:
"I am the LORD, who made all things,
who stretched out the heavens alone,
who spread out the earth —
Who was with me? —
[25]who frustrates the omens of liars,
and makes fools of diviners;
who turns wise men back,
and makes their knowledge foolish;
[26]who confirms the word of his servant,
and performs the counsel of his messengers;
who says of Jerusalem, 'She shall be inhabited,'
and of the cities of Judah, 'They shall be built,
and I will raise up their ruins';
[27]who says to the deep, 'Be dry,
I will dry up your rivers';
[28]who says of Cyrus, 'He is my shepherd,
and he shall fulfil all my purpose';
saying of Jerusalem, 'She shall be built,'
and of the temple, 'Your foundation shall be laid.'"

45 Thus says the LORD to his anointed, to Cyrus,
whose right hand I have grasped,
to subdue nations before him
and ungird the loins of kings,
to open doors before him
that gates may not be closed:
[2]"I will go before you
and level the mountains,
I will break in pieces the doors of bronze
and cut asunder the bars of iron,
[3]I will give you the treasures of darkness
and the hoards in secret places,
that you may know that it is I, the LORD,
the God of Israel, who call you by your name.

[4]For the sake of my servant Jacob,
and Israel my chosen,
I call you by your name,
I surname you, though you do not know me.
[5]I am the LORD, and there is no other,
besides me there is no God;
I gird you, though you do not know me,
[6]that men may know, from the rising of the sun
and from the west, that there is none besides me;
I am the LORD, and there is no other.
[7]I form light and create darkness,
I make weal and create woe,
I am the LORD, who do all these things.

These verses form an independent unit introduced by the messenger formula, "Thus says the Lord," to which two present participles rendered by "your redeemer....who formed you," are attached. The statement "I am Yahweh" is followed immediately by a succession of nine present participles in agreement with Yahweh. In all then Yahweh is qualified by eleven participles — redeeming, fashioning, making, stretching, spreading out, frustrating, turning back, confirming, saying (3 times). This is typical of hymns of descriptive praise. The succession of participles has the effect of creating a tension, holding up the mention of Cyrus as long as possible. The messenger formula is resumed in 45:1 to prepare for the direct address to Cyrus. The audience of course is the community in exile and the address to Cyrus a literary fiction; there is no question of the prophet confronting the king face to face. "All the major elements of the prophecy are present in the introduction: redemption, creation, history, prophecy, sovereignty, and purpose" (J. Muilenburg).

v. 24. The expressions used here are typical of the prophet and have already been explained: *cf.,* 40:22; 41:14; 42:5; 44:2. Hebrew has no single word for the universe or cosmos; "(the) all" of 24b approaches this most closely. At creation Yahweh was "alone....who was with me?" We look here into the depths of the mystery which God is.

vv. 25-26. The creator is always the lord of history. Hundreds of Assyrian and Babylonian tablets have been discovered in recent decades bearing oracles favouring these powers; they are all oracles of salvation, none of adversity, but have been proved futile by the fall of both empires. Yahweh has shown the omens of the fulsome talkers to be vain and has made the diviners act like madmen. Yahweh and he alone, through his messengers, can foretell the course of history. "His servant" of v. 26 is most likely prophetic Israel and evokes Amos 3:7, "Surely the Lord God does nothing without revealing his secret to his servants the prophets." "The counsel of his messengers" is Yahweh's counsel which the prophets announce and which he confirms by action.

v. 27. The "deep" and its "rivers" are the primeval waters. There are many mythological references and allusions in Second Isaiah and this verse is in the same line as 51:9-10. It was Yahweh who controlled the formless and chaotic waters at the beginning and brought cosmos out of chaos.

v. 28. The same God who addresses the primeval chaos as creator now addresses Cyrus as lord of history. He is the master of nature and of history. Yahweh is Israel's shepherd (*cf.*, 40:11 for use of the shepherd imagery); now it is Cyrus who is Yahweh's instrument to carry out his will by ordering Jerusalem to be rebuilt and the Temple to be restored. It would have shocked the exiles to hear a pagan king addressed by Yahweh's title. A number of commentators reject the last half of the verse on the grounds that Second Isaiah shows no interest elsewhere in the Temple. But part of the tragedy of 587 was precisely the destruction of the Temple, and an important part of the restoration would be its re-building. Such a reason for rejecting the half-verse is inadequate in itself.

45:1-7. Now comes the formal oracle addressed, by literary fiction, to Cyrus. The form is very like that of the ritual of the installation of the king in Pss 2; 110(109). Cyrus is Yahweh's anointed, v. 1; Yahweh takes his right hand, v. 1;

calls him by name, vv. 3b and 4b; gives him another name, v. 4b; girds (arms) him, v. 5b. Comparisons have been made between the language of the oracle and that of the Cyrus cylinder (*ANET*, 315-316) on which Marduk is described as calling Cyrus. The cylinder is later than Cyrus so there can be no questions of dependence. It would be an exaggeration to see any more than a general resemblance between the prophetic text and the Cylinder in the areas of common ancient Near Eastern court style and semitic idiom. The reasons for which Yahweh has chosen Cyrus are given in vv. 3b and 4a. The phrase "I am Yahweh" occurs in vv. 3c, 5a, 6c, 7c, and there is further monotheistic emphasis in vv. 5a-b, 6, 7.

v. 1. It is more likely that the verse should read: "Thus says the Lord: 'To his anointed, to Cyrus, whose right hand. . . .'" That is, all of v. 1 after the opening formula would be like the form of address at the opening of a letter. It would be a further shock to the exiles to hear Cyrus addressed as "the anointed one," in Hebrew *messiah* and in Greek *christos*. This was the title of the reigning Hebrew king, given to him at his installation, Ps 2:2, and constituting him as Yahweh's vice-regent. It would be very misleading to read back into the text inter-testamental and New Testament ideas of Messiah. The phrase, "ungird the loins of kings," means to disarm them.

vv. 2-3. The Greek historian Herodotus (5th c. B.C.), 1, 179, mentions 100 gates of bronze around the city of Babylon. The "treasures of darkness. . . ." are treasures hidden away.

vv. 4-5. Cyrus is Yahweh's unknowing instrument; all unknowing he acts for Israel. What Yahweh once did through Judah's kings he now does through a pagan king. Yahweh is not restoring Israel as a political power, but as his servant, described in the servant songs. The phrases, "my servant," "my chosen one," are a constant theme of Second Isaiah: 41:8; 42:1; 43:10; 44:1-2; 49:3-6.

vv. 6-7. Once again there is the assertion that Yahweh is the only one, "there is none but me alone. . . I am Yahweh, there is no other." The purpose of his action through Cyrus is that the whole world may know this. Yahweh is "shaping light, creating darkness, making prosperity, creating adversity." The three verbs are used in the two creation narratives in Gen 1:1-2:4a; 2:4b-25. To see here a polemic against Zoroastrian dualism, the two principles of good and evil, or a divergence from Gen 1:4, where God created only light is, I submit, to follow a false trail. The opposites, light-darkness, prosperity-adversity (lit. shalom-evil), are typical Old Testament, and indeed ancient Near Eastern and Egyptian, usages of the two extremes to express the whole. That this is the meaning is confirmed by v. 7c, "I am the Lord, who do (make) all these things." The verse recalls Amos 3:6b, "Does evil befall a city unless the Lord has done it?" Everything is under the control of the one God who directs history as he will.

45:8
CONCLUDING CRY OF JOY

Shower gently, O heavens, from above,
and let the skies drip down righteousness (*sedeq*);
Let the earth be opened that salvation (*yešaʿ*)
may blossom and prosperity (*sedaqah*) bud together.
I, Yahweh, have created it.

(translation by author)

Some consider this verse a fragment inserted by a later disciple or editor. In its present setting it is a cry of exultant anticipation of God's action. Three key words occur together: *sedeq* is Yahweh's salvific activity; *yesaʿ* is salvation; *sedaqah* is the result of Yahweh's saving action, namely prosperity, and in Ps 85(84):9-13 where steadfast love and faithfulness, righteousness and peace meet, where faithfulness buds from the ground and righteousness (God's activity) stoops down from heaven. In Isa 45:8 creation, salvific activity and prosperity are linked. The rain and the dew were essential to life in the ancient Near East as they are today. When they came in their due time, there was prosperity in the land. Perhaps too there is a polemic against Baal, the Canaanite lord of the storm and rain. It is Yahweh, not Baal who controls the elements; look, Yahweh created it all!

45:9-13.
DO NOT DISPUTE WITH THE CREATOR AND LORD OF HISTORY

[9]"Woe to him who strives with his Maker,
an earthen vessel with the potter!
Does the clay say to him who fashions it,
'What are you making'?
or 'Your work has no handles'?
[10]Woe to him who says to a father,
What are you begetting?'
or to a woman, 'With what are you in travail?'"
[11]Thus says the LORD,
the Holy One of Israel, and his Maker:
"Will you question me about my children,
or command me concerning the work of my hands?
[12]I made the earth,
and created man upon it;
it was my hands that stretched out the heavens,
and I commanded all their host.
[13]I have aroused him in righteousness,
and I will make straight all his ways;
he shall build my city
and set my exiles free,
not for price or reward,"
says the LORD of hosts.

Some exegetes, like C. Westermann, regard the passage as the result of a very complicated process of editing of originally disparate pieces, while J. Muilenburg writes that "the strophe is beautifully constructed." The exiles, shocked by the prophecy that immediately precedes, have asked: how can a pagan king be Yahweh's shepherd, his anointed one, the one who is to free Israel? this is impossible! These verses are the reply. Israel can no more contest Yahweh's decision than a piece of pottery contest the intention of its potter or children the procreative act of parents.

vv. 9-10. The image of the potter at work was part of every day life in the ancient Near East and in Israel in particular, *cf.,* Isa 19:16; Jer 18; 19. The one who disputes with his master — what is he but a piece of common pottery, a fragment among the most common of shattered vessels. The last part of v. 9 is best rendered: "of the finished work, that he has no skill." In v. 10 the context requires "his father" and "his mother."

v. 11. The verse is difficult. The slight emendation which is the basis of the RSV translation makes good sense and good parallelism. Following the Isaiah manuscript from the Dead Sea, one may translate: "Thus says the Lord: the Holy One of Israel, who fashions the future: 'ask me about my children! will you. . . . " The imperative "ask" would be said in irony or, as a parallel to the future in the second part of the verse, be itself read as a future. Yahweh has other children besides Israel; all are his children — did he not create them all, and can he not make use of them as he will?

vv. 12-13. Yahweh is the creator of the world and of all who live in it. His choice cannot be questioned. The first person singular of the pronoun is repeated three times at the beginning of vv.1 2a, 12b, 13a. "It is I who made. . . It is I who stretched out. . . . It is I who aroused him (Cyrus) in my saving purpose (*b^e^sedeq*)." Yahweh is solely responsible; the whole passage is completely theocentric. Yahweh has a plan of salvation, 42:6, and "it is he (Cyrus). . . . " who will carry it out. Some commentators have difficulty in reconciling "not for price or reward" with 43:3 and 45:14. But Cyrus is not Yahweh's mercenary; he is his instrument. On the scale of world history, the restoration of the exiles is but an insignificant event, a by-product of his more spectacular military campaigns. All his other conquests later fell into other hands and eventually faded, but Israel is still there, ironically as a non-political force. He won the rewards of his military conquests, but nothing for setting Israel free.

45:14-25.
YAHWEH, THE ONE, ONLY GOD, CREATOR, SAVIOUR AND DELIVERER

[14]Thus says the LORD:
"The wealth of Egypt and the merchandise of Ethiopia,
and the Sa.be'ans, men of stature,
shall come over to you and be yours,
they shall follow you;
they shall come over in chains and bow down to you.
They will make supplication to you, saying:
'God is with you only, and there is no other,
no god besides him.'"
[15]Truly, thou art a God who hidest thyself,
O God of Israel, the Saviour.
[16]All of them are put to shame and confounded,
the makers of idols go in confusion together.
[17]But Israel is saved by the LORD
with everlasting salvation;
you shall not be put to shame or confounded
to all eternity.

[18]For thus says the LORD,
who created the heavens
he is God!,
who formed the earth and made it
he established it;
he did not create it a chaos,
he formed it to be inhabited!:
"I am the LORD, and there is no other.
[19]I did not speak in secret,
in a land of darkness;
I did not say to the offspring of Jacob,
'Seek me in chaos.'
I the LORD speak the truth,
I declare what is right.

[20]"Assemble yourselves and come,
draw near together,
you survivors of the nations!

They have no knowledge
who carry about their wooden idols,
and keep on praying to a god
that cannot save.
21 Declare and present your case;
let them take counsel together!
Who told this long ago?
Who declared it of old?
Was it not I, the LORD?
And there is no other god besides me,
a righteous God and a Saviour;
there is none besides me.

22 "Turn to me and be saved,
all the ends of the earth!
For I am God, and there is no other.
23 By myself I have sworn,
from my mouth has gone forth in righteousness
a word that shall not return:
'To me every knee shall bow,
every tongue shall swear.'

24 "Only in the LORD, it shall be said of me,
are righteousness and strength;
to him shall come and be ashamed,
all who were incensed against him.
25 In the LORD all the offspring of Israel
shall triumph and glory."

A number of exegetes find vv. 14-17 to be a series of fragments with no connection at all with each other and contend that each fragment is to be examined in itself, be there two, vv. 14-15 and 16-17 or three, 14, 15, and 16-17. The particle "for" in v. 18 is often regarded as an editorial link which ties the disconnected fragments with what follows. Others are of the opinion that there is unity in the passage and that vv. 14-15 "represents a peak of theological and poetic intensity. . . . the themes of the absolute and unique divinity of Yahweh and the unity of mankind under the sovereignty of Yahweh" (J. L. McKenzie), and that "to appreciate the quality of the poet's thought it is necessary to cast aside all literalistic interpretations" (J. Muilenburg). These two authors point in the right direction.

Even though fragments may have been brought together here, it is the text that lies before us that is the subject for exegesis, not some scholarly construct. Nor is the poet's logic necessarily ours.

These twelve verses persistently assert the uniqueness of Israel's God: "God is with you only, and there is no other...," 14a; "Yahweh.... *he* is God," 18a; "I, Yahweh, and there is no other," 18d; "I Yahweh...," 19c; "Was it not I, Yahweh, and there is no other God besides me...," 21c; ".... none apart from me," 21d; "for I am God, and there is no other," 22b; "only in Yahweh...," 24a; "in Yahweh...," 25. These repeated monotheistic assertions, nine of them, have a cumulative effect. Accompanying them is the word "save" which appears six times as a noun/participle or a verb: "God of Israel, saviour," 15; "Israel is saved by Yahweh with an everlasting salvation," 17; the pagans invoke "a god who does not save," 20c; Yahweh is a "god who delivers and saves," 21d; the pagans are invited to "turn to me and be saved," 22a. The word "save" has not yet the overtones of the Christian theology of the New Testament; the basic meaning is that Yahweh will vindicate his people in the eyes of their enemies who will be brought to acknowledge the God of Israel in act.

Forms of the word *sedeq*, "righteousness," with its various emphases on Yahweh's saving action and its effects, occurs five times: "I, Yahweh, who speak order, declare what is proper," 19b; "God deliverer, yes and saviour," 21d; "due order has gone forth from my mouth...," 23a; "only in Yahweh....are saving acts and might," 24a; "in Yahweh alone all the descendants of Israel shall prosper...," 25. Yahweh's action towards the world looks to due order, to his people and to their well being.

Finally, besides the proper name for the God of Israel, Yahweh, and the ordinary word for God, Elohim, there occurs five times *El*. *El* is the general and ancient semitic word for God, in particular for "the high god"; it is found in Akkadian, Ugaritic, Phoenician. It was the name of the senior god of the Canaanite pantheon. "With you only is *El*," 14d; "truly you are a hidden *El*," 15; the pagans "pray to an El who cannot save," 20c; "Yahweh is. . . . *El*, deliverer and saviour," 21d; "I am El, there is no other," 22b. These are yet further monotheistic assertions; the only one who has claim to be "the high God" is the unique God of Israel, besides whom there is no other.

On the grounds of rhetorical criticism and because of these themes which run throughout, vv. 14-15 will be considered as a unity as it lies before us, whatever the origin of some of its parts may be.

vv. 14-15. The oracle speaks of a religious, not of a military, submission. The three African nations are those mentioned in 43:3-4; Cyrus has conquered them and they now submit themselves spiritually to Israel. The first two nouns referring to Egypt and Ethiopia are abstracts for the concrete and are to be rendered "toilers" and "merchants," parallel with the "tall Sabeans" (lit. "men of stature"). The verb "come (pass) over" has resonances of making a pilgrimage (*cf.*, Isa 2:1-4; 60; 66:18-23), and "they shall follow you," (lit. "they shall go after you"), echoes the cultic expression of Deuteronomy to go after Yahweh or strange gods.

The prophet, or Israel, then exclaims, "Truly you are a hidden God. . . ," an acknowledgement that God's action in liberating Israel through the conquests of a pagan king is hidden and only comes to light later. C. Westermann considers the verse to be an "Amen" gloss, *i.e.*, the later addition of a scribe who signifies his approval of what is being said. The slight emendation of the 2nd person singular pronoun "you" to "with you" to give "God is hidden with you" is based on less than the flimsiest textual evidence. These verses are outright monotheistic assertions.

vv. 16-17. "The hewers of idols" in Babylon will be put to shame and confusion when they witness the submission of the African nations. But Israel will not be put to shame and confusion because her lasting salvation is with Yahweh. A number of commentators understand v. 16 as a sudden reference to idol makers to be read with 44:9 & 20 — an originally independent unit inserted here out of context.

vv. 18-19. It is generally maintained that "for" is a connecting particle inserted by an editor to join this independent, perhaps fragmentary, piece with what precedes. The passage, vv. 18-19, is complete in itself. The beginning is typical of the hymns of descriptive praise and this is seen more clearly when the participles are given their full value: ". . . . Yahweh, creator of the heavens, he is God, former and maker of the earth, he set it firm." The forceful noun clause at the end of v. 18a, "he God." is an assertion of uniqueness. God has a purpose in creation; he did not create the world a chaos, *tohû*, but to be lived in. *Tohû* is the direct opposite of creation. In its 20 uses in the Old Testament it describes grim desert, waste, devastation; it also means nothingness. In the creation passage in Gen 1:2 it describes, with the alliterative *bohû*, "before creation," *i.e.* the opposite of meaningful and ordered existence. "I, Yahweh. . . ," — a monotheistic assertion — am responsible for this order. Verse 19 has given rise to various interpretations. The majority think that the God of Israel is saying that he does not speak in the obscure, esoteric mumblings of pseudo-prophets, magicians or sorcerers; many are of the opinion that the phrase, "in a land of darkness," may well refer to Sheol and the necromancers, *cf.*, 1 Sam 28. But the language of vv. 18-19 is that of the creation narratives of Gen 1:1-3 and Gen 2:4-7, as is the language of 45:6-7. (This is not to maintain that Second Isaiah knew the creation narratives in the precise form in which they now lie before us. The formulas were already part of Israelite tradition.) Yahweh is creator, former, maker; darkness and *tohû* are part of the description of chaos, "before creation," in Gen 1:2. He is saying, do not seek me in *tohû*, pre-creation chaos; chaos and wind, mentioned together in Gen 1:2, are the gods of the pagans, "their works are nothing, their molten images wind and chaos (*tohû*)," Isa 41:29. God is not found there; that is the realm whence the pagan non-entities arose; he is found in the order and stability which comes from his word. In Gen 1, God spoke, and it was so; God is found in his word which speaks order. Verse 19 ends with another monotheistic assertion — "I, Yahweh, speaking order, declaring what is proper." God is found in world order; his word and action are one. In Ps 9:8 Yahweh judges the world "in [good] order" and "as is proper," the same two Hebrew words.

vv. 20-21. These verses introduce a disputation passage which, however, must be read within the context of vv. 14-15. The "survivors of the nations," that is the pagans who have lived through Cyrus' conquests, are summoned to state a case for themselves. They are described as those who cannot experience (know) Yahweh's action, because they walk in procession after an *El* who cannot save, v. 20c; whereas Yahweh is an *El* saviour, and there is none besides him. Let the pagans take counsel as they may, says the judge, and it will be found that Yahweh alone has foretold all this, namely what is happening now through Cyrus. The verses are a summons to court to see who is the source of salvation — "a righteous God and saviour"; righeous, *saddîq*, is determined by context and by "saviour"; it describes Yahweh in act as saviour, "*El* deliverer, yes and saviour," 21d.

vv. 22-23, 24-25. If Yahweh is the only saviour, then creation and all that is in it, "all the ends of the earth," must turn to him, because he is El who stands alone. Yahweh then affirms on solemn oath that there is perfect correspondence between his word and deed, v. 23a: "due order has gone forth from my mouth, a word that shall surely not return." Verse 23b runs on into v. 24a: confronted with what has gone before "every knee shall bend to me, every tongue shall swear, 'only in Yahweh, be it said, are saving acts and might.'" The plural of *sedaqah* is rendered "saving acts" as in Judg 5:11; Mic 6:5; Ps 71(70):19. The might is the power that brings the saving acts into effect. Those shamed, *cf.*, v. 16, and incensed against Yahweh will come and adhere to him. Israel then will prosper (the verb of *sedeq*) and glory —not in political power, but in Yahweh.

Claus Westermann has noted how vv. 23b-24a have been taken up in the New Testament, Rom 14:11, Phil 2:10f, in the strict sense of the original. All are invited to acknowledge and take part in God's saving action; those who freely discover that he alone is God can become members of the people of God. Israel and the Church are religious, not political bodies.

46:1-13.
THE GODS ARE POWERLESS, BUT YAHWEH ALL POWERFUL

46 Bēl bows down, Nē'bō stoops,
their idols are on beasts and cattle;
these things you carry are loaded
as burdens on weary beasts.
[2]They stoop, they bow down together,
they cannot save the burden,
but themselves go into captivity.

[3]"Hearken to me, O house of Jacob,
all the remnant of the house of Israel,
who have been borne by me from your birth,
carried from the womb;
[4]even to your old age I am He,
and to gray hairs I will carry you.
I have made, and I will bear;
I will carry and will save.

[5]"To whom will you liken me and make me equal,
and compare me, that we may be alike?
[6]Those who lavish gold from the purse,
and weigh out silver in the scales,
hire a goldsmith, and he makes it into a god;
then they fall down and worship!
[7]They lift it upon their shoulders, they carry it,
they set it in its place, and it stands there;

it cannot move from its place.
If one cries to it, it does not answer
or save him from his trouble.
[8]"Remember this and consider,
recall it to mind, you transgressors,
[9]remember the former things of old;
for I am God, and there is no other;
I am God, and there is none like me,
[10]declaring the end from the beginning
and from ancient times things not yet done,
saying, 'My counsel shall stand,
and I will accomplish all my purpose,'
[11]calling a bird of prey from the east,
the man of my counsel from a far country.
I have spoken, and I will bring it to pass;
I have purposed, and I will do it.

[12]"Hearken to me, you stubborn of heart,
you who are far from deliverance:
[13]I bring near my deliverance, it is not far off,
and my salvation will not tarry;
I will put salvation in Zion,
for Israel my glory."

The passage is treated as a unity, though vv. 5-7(8) are rather loosely joined to the context. In vv. 1-4 the Babylonians carry their gods whereas Yahweh carries his people; vv. 5-7 take up 40:18, 25 and return to the theme of idol making and casting; vv. 8-13 resume history, prophecy and fulfilment through Yahweh's saving action. The verses are firmly clamped to 45:18-25; in fact C. Westermann considered 45:18—46:13 (omitting 46:4-8) as a single unit divided by interrelated imperatives, vv. 3, 9, 12.

vv. 1-4. The prophet anticipates in imagination the fall of Babylon. With the Persian attack imminent, the Babylonians load the images of their gods on to animals, and so the prophet can say, "their images are given over to (become the property of) beast and animal, carried as loads on weary beasts of burden." Bel, the cognate of the Hebrew Baal, was

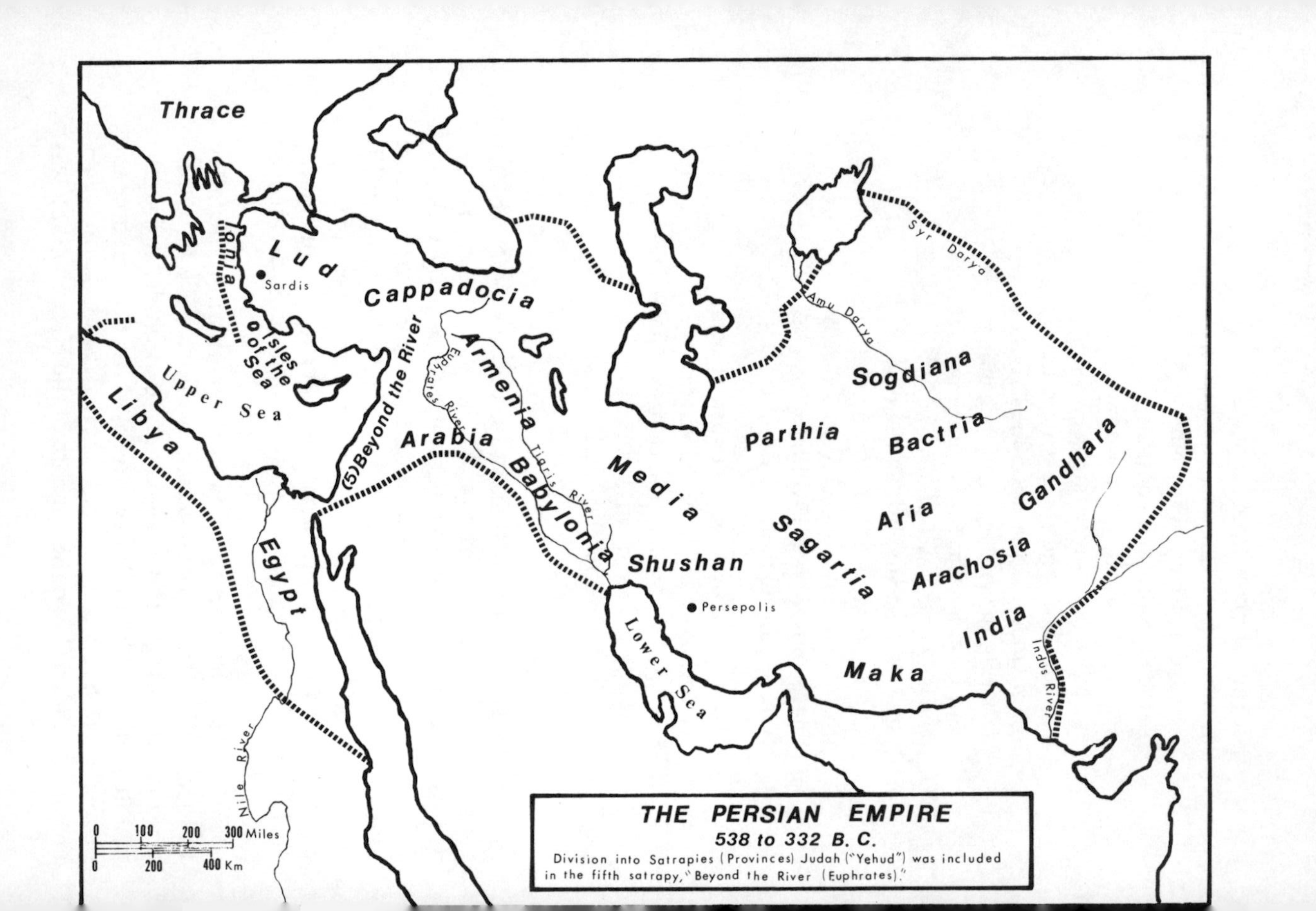
THE PERSIAN EMPIRE
538 to 332 B. C.
Division into Satrapies (Provinces) Judah ("Yehud") was included in the fifth satrapy, "Beyond the River (Euphrates)."
Thrace
Ionia
Lud
Sardis
Cappadocia
Isles of the Sea
Upper Sea
Libya
(5) Beyond the River
Armenia
Euphrates River
Tigris River
Arabia
Babylonia
Egypt
Nile River
Media
Shushan
Persepolis
Lower Sea
Parthia
Sagartia
Sogdiana
Bactria
Aria
Arachosia
Gandhara
India
Maka
Syr Darya
Amu Darya
Indus River
0 100 200 300 Miles
0 200 400 Km

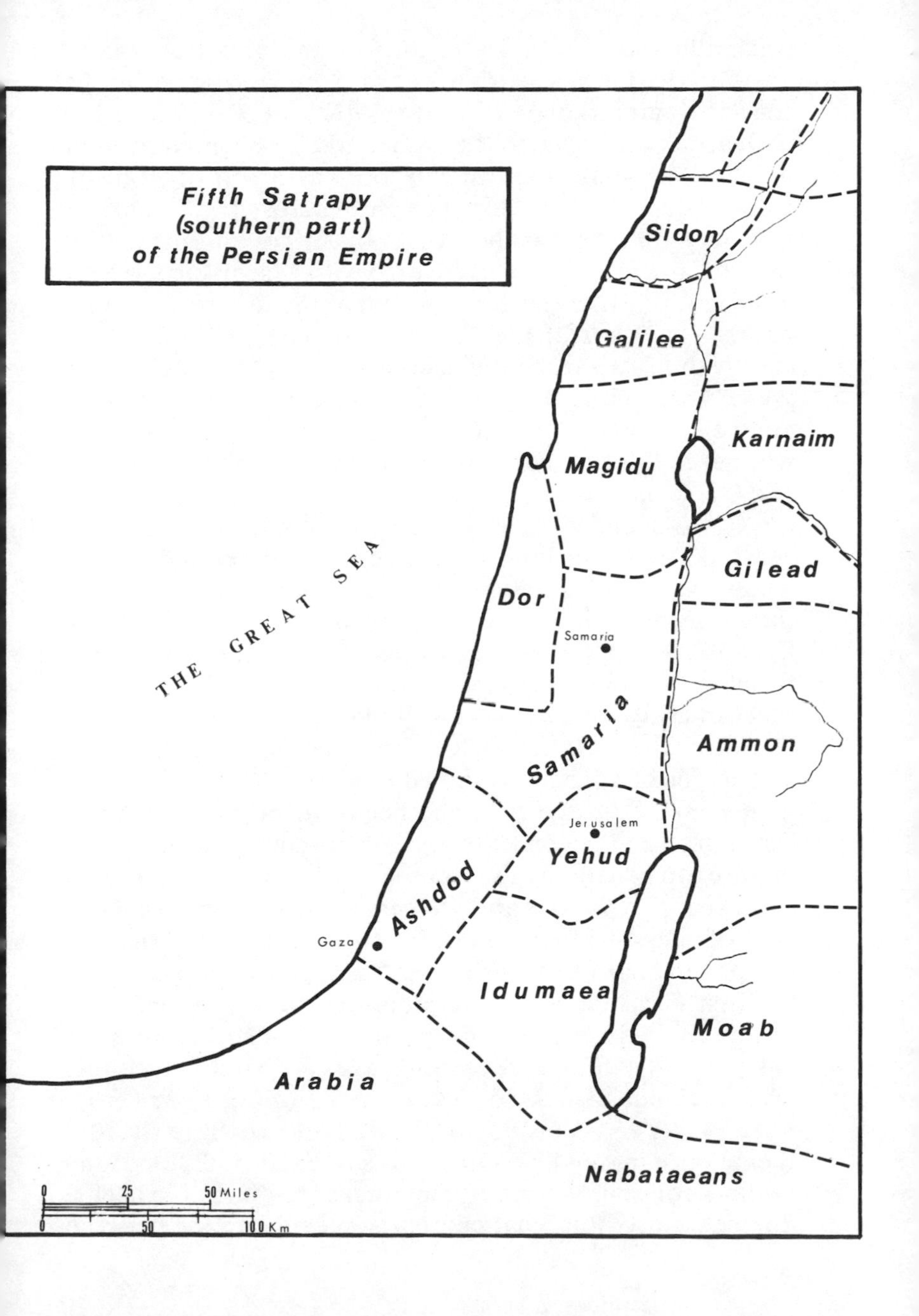
Fifth Satrapy
(southern part)
of the Persian Empire
Sidon
Galilee
Karnaim
Magidu
Gilead
Dor
THE GREAT SEA
Samaria
Samaria
Ammon
Jerusalem
Yehud
Ashdod
Gaza
Idumaea
Moab
Arabia
Nabataeans
0
25
50 Miles
0
50
100 Km

originally the title of Enlil, lord of the upper air and a creation deity whosc shrine was at Nippur; later, from the time of Hammurabi (c. 1728-1686), the title was transferred to Marduk and became the name most frequently given to him in Akkadian literature. Nebo was a son of Marduk whose temple was at Borsippa, just across the Euphrates from Babylon; he was the patron of scribes and the god of wisdom and was closely associated with Marduk in the New Year liturgy. His name formed part of the throne name of a number of rulers of the Chaldean dynasty, 625-538 B.C., *e.g.* Nabopolassar, Nebuchadnezzar, Nabonidus. These gods, representing Babylon, fall with the city. They crouch and cower as they go into captivity. This picture however was never realized; Babylon fell peacefully and bloodlessly, and Cyrus paid due homage to Bel and Nebo, as we read on the Cyrus cylinder: ". . . . I resettled upon the command of Marduk, the great lord, all the gods of Sumer and Akkad whom Narbonidus has brought into Babylon. . . . may all the gods whom I have resettled in their sacred cities daily ask Bel and Nebo for a long life for me. . . . " (*ANET*, 316). But this does not blunt the sharpness of the prophet's thrust. In times of crises the devotees carry the images of their gods, in fact carry the gods themselves; but Israel's God carries her. The words of v. 1b are resumed in v. 3b. Yahweh has been with Israel from the time she began to be a nation right through to and beyond the present, though great faith was required to adhere to this after the trauma of the destruction and exile. The phrases and imagery are traditional: Isa 44:2, 24; 49:5; Deut 1:31; Hos 11:3; Isa 40:11; 63:9. In v. 4 the first person singular of the pronoun, "I," is repeated five times, the first occasion being the monotheistic assertion "I am he," echoing the previous chapter. Yahweh has acted in the past; he will continue to act and save, v. 4b, and this is just what the gods of Babylon were unable to do, v. 2b.

vv. 5-7. Verse 5 resumes 40:18, 25 and we have the idol theme once more (40:18-19; 41:6-7; 44:9-20; 45:20b). Many authors consider the passage an interpolation and in itself a dubious unity. But what comparison can there be between the incomparable Yahweh and a thing that people commission gold- and silversmiths to fashion! People fall down before the work of human hands; they have to pick it up, lump it around, set it down; it cannot save, cannot answer prayers, *cf.,* 45:20b.

vv. 8-11. The transgressors, namely the exiles, are summoned to remember that their one and only God is the God of history; he alone has foretold in the past and brought to fulfilment; he alone controls history. And that is what he is doing now: "declaring. . . . saying. . . . calling. . . ." He summons Cyrus as a "bird of prey" who will carry out his plan. Israel's God appeals to tradition in vv. 9-10, not to some static thing in the past, but to something living out of the past in the present, to the nation's continual experience of God in history. As a recent writer has said in another context, "Tradition is not the past, it is the Church's self-consciousness *now* of that which has been handed on to her not as an inert treasure but as a dynamic inner life" (Robert Taft, *Worship*, 55[1981]3). In v. 11b God stresses in impassioned rhetoric and by means of a three times repeated emphatic particle that he has acted in the past and will continue to act into the future.

vv. 12-13. This is a further summons to Israel, "stubborn of heart." Yahweh's "deliverance" (*sedaqah*) is his saving action which will restore Israel and adorn her (this is not the glory, *kābôd*, of God's abiding presence, but an adornment which he puts on Israel).

47:1-15.
THE FALL OF BABYLON

47 Come down and sit in the dust,
O virgin daughter of Babylon;
sit on the ground without a throne
O daughter of the Chaldeans!
For you shall no more be called
tender and delicate.

[2]Take the millstone and grind meal,
put off your veil,
strip off your robe, uncover your legs,
pass through the rivers.
[3]Your nakedness shall be uncovered,
and your shame shall be seen.
I will take vengeance,
and I will spare no man.
[4]Our Redeemer — the LORD of hosts is his name —
is the Holy One of Israel.

[5]Sit in silence, and go into darkness,
O daughter of the Chaldeans;
for you shall no more be called
the mistress of kingdoms.
[6]I was angry with my people,
I profaned my heritage;
I gave them into your hand,
you showed them no mercy;
on the aged you made your yoke
exceedingly heavy.
[7]You said, "I shall be mistress for ever,"
so that you did not lay these things to heart
or remember their end.

[8]Now therefore hear this, you lover of pleasures,
who sit securely,
who say in your heart,
"I am, and there is no one besides me;
I shall not sit as a widow
or know the loss of children":
[9]These two things shall come to you
in a moment, in one day;
the loss of children and widowhood
shall come upon you in full measure,
in spite of your many sorceries
and the great power of your enchantments.

[10]You felt secure in your wickedness,
you said, "No one sees me";

your wisdom and your knowledge
 led you astray,
and you said in your heart,
 "I am, and there is no one besides me."
[11]But evil shall come upon you,
 for which you cannot atone;
disaster shall fall upon you,
 which you will not be able to expiate;
and ruin shall come on you suddenly,
 of which you know nothing.

[12]Stand fast in your enchantments
 and your many sorceries,
 with which you have labored from your youth;
perhaps you may be able to succeed,
 perhaps you may inspire terror.
[13]You are wearied with your many counsels;
 let them stand forth and save you,
those who divide the heavens,
 who gaze at the stars,
who at the new moons predict
 what shall befall you.

[14]Behold, they are like stubble,
 the fire consumes them;
they cannot deliver themselves
 from the power of the flame.
No coal for warming oneself is this,
 no fire to sit before!
[15]Such to you are those with whom you have labored,
 who have trafficked with you from your youth;
they wander about each in his own direction;
 there is no one to save you.

We move from the demise of the gods of Babylon to the demise of the city. The passage, which is a unity, has often been described as comprising elements from a "mocking song" and a "triumphal song." But these terms are not appropriate. It belongs rather to the group of "oracles against the nations," Isa 13-23; Jer 46-51; Ezek 25-32, and in some of the minor prophets. There were a number of such oracles current against Babylon, Isa 13-14; Jer 50-51. The prophet is proclaiming the fall of Babylon and its empire before the event. The speaker throughout is Yahweh and the skillfully contrived poem moves through six stophes: vv. 1-4, the lady who lived in luxury is to be humiliated and degraded; vv. 5-7, she has been a pitiless tyrant; vv. 8-9, she will become widow and childless; vv. 10-11, her knowledge and pride cannot avert disaster; vv. 12-13, magic and astrology are helpless; vv. 14-15, those who traffic with her have only self-interest at heart.

vv. 1-4. "Get down" is a better rendering than "come down." "Virgin daughter" is addressed to Israel in Jer 31:4, 21; Amos 5:2, and to Egypt in Jer 46:11, referring to one as yet unconquered and unravished. She who has been pampered (almost "well-fed") must stoop to the lowest of manual labour, turning the mill-stone. She must uncover her (plaited) tresses, strip off her long veil (or train), bare her thighs. Middle Eastern and Egyptian art carry portraits of women working in such a state. She will be raped — this is the meaning in the context of "your nakedness will be uncovered." Yahweh will take vengeance, he will be inexorable, "I will parley with no man" (C. R. North). The end of v. 3 and v. 4 hang together only with difficulty. An emendation gives ". . . . says our Redeemer, Yahweh of hosts. . . ."

vv. 5-7. Babylon passes from glory and acclamation to darkness and silence. She is no longer "Queen of the kingdoms." Yahweh, the lord of history, delivered Israel into the hands of Babylon, and Babylon did not recognize this (how could she?). In fact Babylon's hand was not all that harsh over captive Israel — if, of course, captivity can be anything other than harsh. But it is Babylon's arrogance that is to be punished. How could any nation claim to exercise power for ever?

vv. 8-9. When Babylon says, "I am, and there is no one besides me," then this is a blasphemous usurpation of Yahweh's claim to be unique, *cf.*, 45:5, 6, 18, 22; 46:9. She is complacent in her superiority and self-trust, but has not reckoned, has not known how many disastrous events will "come" upon her; this note is sounded five times, vv. 9a, 9b, 11a, 11c, 13c. Second Isaiah regards sorcery, magic and astrology as an essential ingredient of Babylonian religion, and returns to the theme in vv. 12-13.

vv. 10-11. Babylon considered herself beyond the all-seeing eye of the divinity, a familiar image in the ancient Near East, especially in Egypt. And further, her intellectual and cultural advance, "your wisdom and your knowledge," led her to *hybris* and usurpation of the divine, "I am...," *cf.*, v. 8. She felt secure in her wickedness, *ra'ah*; but the same Hebrew word also means evil, and evil shall come upon her, v. 11, and disaster overtake her before she knows what is happening.

vv. 12-13. The archaeological discoveries of the last century or more have provided an abundance of magical, astrological and astronomical texts from Mesopotamia. The diviners studied the movements of the heavens so as to predict and control events on earth; the scholars plotted the courses of the heavenly bodies and so foretold the future. The diviner and the scholar were sometimes one and the same. But no longer can Babylon have confidence in her possession of this knowledge. The God of Israel alone can foretell the future because he is the lord of history.

vv. 14-15. Babylon will be consumed by fire, and it will not be a gentle fire before which one can warm oneself, *cf.* 44:16. Those who have had commercial dealings with Babylon, "who trafficked with you from your youth," have only their own interest at heart; they cannot help; no-one, nothing, neither their gods nor their science and knowledge nor their business partners, can save Babylon, a theme constantly recurring in these chapters, *cf.*, 45:16; 46:2, 6, 7, 13; 47:13b.

48:1-22.
PROPHECY AND HISTORY

48 Hear this, O house of Jacob,
who are called by the name of Israel,
and who came forth from the loins of Judah;
who swear by the name of the LORD,
and confess the God of Israel,
but not in truth or right.
[2]For they call themselves after the holy city,
and stay themselves on the God of Israel;
the LORD of hosts is his name.

[3]"The former things I declared of old,
they went forth from my mouth and I made them known;
then suddenly I did them and they came to pass.
[4]Because I know that you are obstinate,
and your neck is an iron sinew
and your forehead brass,
[5]I declared them to you from of old,
before they came to pass I announced them to you,
lest you should say, 'My idol did them,
my graven image and my molten image commanded them.'

[6]"You have heard; now see all this;
and will you not declare it?
From this time forth I make you hear new things,
hidden things which you have not known.
[7]They are created now, not long ago;
before today you have never heard of them,
lest you should say, 'Behold, I knew them.'
[8]You have never heard, you have never known,
from of old your ear has not been opened.
For I knew that you would deal very treacherously,
and that from birth you were called a rebel.

[9]"For my name's sake I defer my anger,
for the sake of my praise I restrain it for you,
that I may not cut you off.

[10]Behold, I have refined you, but not like silver;
I have tried you in the furnace of affliction.
[11]For my own sake, for my own sake, I do it,
for how should my name be profaned?
My glory I will not give to another.

[12]"Hearken to me, O Jacob,
and Israel, whom I called!
I am He, I am the first,
and I am the last.
[13]My hand laid the foundation of the earth,
and my right hand spread out the heavens;
when I call to them,
they stand forth together.

[14]"Assemble, all of you, and hear!
Who among them has declared these things?
The LORD loves him;
he shall perform his purpose on Babylon,
and his arm shall be against the Chaldeans.
[15]I, even I, have spoken and called him,
I have brought him, and he will prosper in his way,
[16]Draw near to me, hear this:
from the beginning I have not spoken in secret,
from the time it came to be I have been there."
And now the LORD GOD has sent me and his Spirit.
[17]Thus says the LORD,
your Redeemer, the Holy One of Israel:
"I am the LORD your God,
who teaches you to profit,
who leads you in the way you should go.
[18]O that you had hearkened to my commandments!
Then your peace would have been like a river,
and your righteousness like the waves of the sea;
[19]your offspring would have been like the sand,
and your descendants like its grains;
their name would never be cut off
or destroyed from before me."

[20]Go forth from Babylon, flee from Chaldea,
declare this with a shout of joy, proclaim it,
send it forth to the end of the earth;
say, "The LORD has redeemed his servant Jacob!"
[21]They thirsted not when he led them through the deserts;
he made water flow for them from the rock;
he cleft the rock and the water gushed out.
[22]"There is no peace," says the LORD, "for the wicked."

The interpretation of this chapter was determined by Bernhard Duhm in his commentary in 1892 and has been followed by virtually every commentator since. According to Duhm, chap. 48, or at least vv. 1-11, was originally a series of coherent utterances on the theme of salvation to which a later hand, not that of Second Isaiah, added the "harsh accusations" against Israel. These harsh additions have no place in the original, according to Claus Westermann, while R. N. Whybray is convinced that the inevitable conclusion is that two types of material have been interwoven. The "salvation themes" would be found in vv. 1a, 3, 5a, 6, 7a, 12-13, 14-16, 20-21; the "harsh additions" would be vv. 1b, 2, 4, 5b, 7b, 8, 9-10(11?), 18, 19, with slight variations according to the different commentators.

James Muilenburg takes a very different view: chap. 48 is one poem in two parts each comprising four strophes and each rising to a climax in the fourth: 1st part, vv. 1-2, 3-5, 6-8, 9-11; 2nd part, vv. 12-13, 14-15, 16-17, 18-19; vv. 20-21 form a lyrical finale and v. 22 is a later addition, *cf.,* 57:21. He draws attention to literary or rhetorical devices such as the recurrence of the verb "to hear" 10 times, and the significance of "word" in biblical thought; of "to call" 6 times, "to speak" twice, "declare" or "tell" 6 times, Jacob 3 times, and "name" 6 times.

It is often said by commentators that the removal of the "harsh additions" from 48:1-11 leaves a well constructed utterance directed to another purpose. But one may ask whether the concept of a "well constructed utterance" is not drawn up under the influence of 19th and 20th century

European literary theories and imposed on a text written in a different culture, without printing press, some 2500 years earlier.

This commentary will try to expound the text as it stands as Scripture and not exegete an allegedly unscrambled version, though difficulties and incoherencies will be pointed out. The text will be considered in four parts, vv. 1-11, 12-16, 17-19, 20-21(22).

The general theme is that Yahweh has long ago foretold the whole history of his people and that his words have been fulfilled. Israel, stubborn from the first, has not given assent to this; but she cannot attribute the direction of history to any idol god. Yahweh is directing the present course of events, including the return home of Jacob under the aegis of a pagan victor, Cyrus. Because of Yahweh's record in the past he should be given credence in the present. This journey back is but a continuation of the first journey and action of God in the desert. He never ceases to act in history. The "first," *i.e.* Yahweh's deeds of old, and the "last," his present deeds, meet and overlap. A number of themes from the previous chapters are drawn together here, especially themes from chaps. 45-47.

vv. 1-11.

vv. 1-2. Yahweh addresses the people as Jacob, Israel, Judah — three names with ancestral, religious and geographical (tribal) history and with associations of election, blessing, solidarity, promises. The context is that of Israel's long tradition of worship; they "swear by the name of Yahweh," *i.e.,* they make religious vows; they "invoke" or "call to remembrance" the God of Israel, *i.e.,* liturgically they make active in the present God's great deeds in the past; "they stay themselves," *i.e.,* they trust in the God of Israel. But they have no right to do all this; their worship through the centuries has not been "in accord with truth, in due order" (*'emet* and *sedaqah*), because their lives have not been lived in accordance with the spirit of their worship.

vv. 3-5. Many regard vv. 4 and 5b as "harsh interpolations." The "former things," *cf.,* 41:22-23; 42:9; 43:9, 19; 46:9-10, indicate the former course of history, which "I declared long ago," vv. 3a and 5a; because this has happened in the past one should therefore accept that the "new things" will happen in the future. The effectiveness of the words going forth from the mouth of God is described in Isa 55:10-11 (*cf.,* comments on 40:1-8). There may be a long time lapse between prediction and fulfilment, but all is in God's hands. He acts suddenly. His experience, "because I know," is that Israel has been an obstinate people from the beginning and has turned to other gods.

vv. 6-8. James Muilenburg has drawn attention to the solemn emphasis on the motif of hearing in these verses; various forms of "to hear" occur 4 times, and of "to know" 4 times. Israel has heard all that has been foretold in the past. She is now called to reflect on it, and then summoned to declare it; v. 6aii is best rendered, "and you, will you not declare it?" In the first part of v. 6, "you" is singular, in the second part, plural. The "new" and "hidden" things which Yahweh now makes her hear are the events beginning with Cyrus' early successes leading to the conquest of Babylon and described through chaps. 40-47. God "creates" new events in history — they were not there before — just as he creates cosmos and nature, v. 7. The effect of the verse is best caught as follows: "Now they are created, no, not long ago, no, not before today, and you have not heard them, lest you might say, yes, I knew them already." A new era in God's action in history is now introduced; Israel could never have heard this from the idols of Babylon, and her ear has never been sufficiently attuned to the word of God in the past. The polemic against her obtuseness is sharp and is hammered out by the three times repeated particle *gam* before a verb: "Never have you heard, never have you known, never has your ear been opened from of old," v. 8a. The traditional theme that she is stubborn from her birth is repeated. It is scarcely to the point to allege an inconsistency between "you have heard . . . ," v. 6a, and "you have never heard . . . ," v. 8a. The poet is saying that Israel has not learnt. The prophecies have pounded on her ears, but she has never given a real assent.

vv. 9-11. Yahweh is long-suffering; he does not cut Israel off, *i.e.*, he does not destroy her according to her deserts, for that would not redound to the glory (praise) of his name, v. 9b. The following verse is difficult, and the RSV, "like silver," is untenable. The "furnace of affliction" or the smelting pot is usually a reference to the bondage in Egypt: Deut 4:20; 1 Kgs 8:51; Jer 11:4. The refining, the assaying, "not in the matter of silver," possibly means "not to get silver from you in the process," but simply to see what is there. One recalls the sentiment of Deut 8:2, "And you shall remember all the way which the Lord your God has led you these forty years in the wilderness, that he might humble you, testing you to know what was in your heart, whether you would keep his commandments or not," a sentiment taken up here in v. 18a. Yahweh is acting salvifically now; his name would be profaned if his action terminated in destruction.

vv. 12-16. God speaks here as 1) the everlasting one, v. 12b, 2) the creator, v. 13, 3) the lord of history, v. 14f, 4) the one who effects the accomplishment of Cyrus' work, v. 14f., 5) the one who does not act in secret, v. 16a. He is the one who ultimately sets the exiles on their way back to Jerusalem. The first pronoun "I" occurs seven times in these verses to stress Yahweh's personal interest and interaction.

vv. 12-13. Yahweh now puts to Jacob/Israel the arguments that he had previously put to the nations in claim of his divinity. She must recognize that he is at work. "I am he, I am the beginning, yes I am the end," v. 12b; the emphasis is on God who is one, unique, eternal. He is the creator and orderer of the cosmos, and it is he who calls Israel. Historical Israel is put in relationship with the creation of the world. It is not helpful to say that Second Isaiah is not preoccupied with creation at the beginning of time. Rather he accepts this tradition as something about which there can be no discussion.

vv. 14-16. The form of disputation appears again. It is not at all certain who are the addressees, though Israel seems most likely. A large number of manuscripts read "who among you" in v. 14b. Neither Israel nor the gods of Babylon could have foretold "these things," Yahweh's new action in history. Yahweh loves Cyrus who has already been called my shepherd, my anointed, the man of my counsel. The Cyrus Cylinder reads: "I am Cyrus. . . . whose rule Bel and Nebo love, whom they want as king to please their hearts. . . (*ANET*, 316). The last part of v. 14 should probably be rendered, "he shall effect his pleasure on Babylon and his power (*lit.*, arm) on the Chaldeans," understanding the preposition with Babylon as a double-duty preposition to be read with the Chaldeans; the RSV is correct. Verse 15 with its pronouns and emphatic particle stresses once more the action of Yahweh. He, the eternal one, has been there ever since anything came to be.

There is no satisfactory explanation of the last part of v. 16. Is it the prophet speaking? is it under the later influence of Isa 61:1? is it a gloss to, a comment on 49:1-6 which has slipped in? Someone is convinced that he has been sent by God and has his Spirit.

vv. 17-19. The oracle formula usually introduces a new section. The titles are already familiar. The participles of descriptive praise are in apposition to the pronoun "I." Yahweh is the one "who makes for you the way along which you are to go." Israel's way home does not lie along the path of military success; it is the minor by-product of the success of a foreign power which is under the hand of Yahweh. The way is both the geographical way back and the way of Israel's conduct. The sentiment of v. 18 is that of Deut 28. With proper observance of the commandments Israel's welfare (*shālôm*) would have been, could still be, like the strongly-flowing Tigris or Euphrates, and not like a Palestinian wadi, her prosperity (*sedaqah*) like the waves of the sea, ever rolling in, as one can observe from any elevated point near the Mediterranean coast. Verse 19 obviously refers to the promise to the patriarchs, *cf.*, Gen 22:17; 32:12.

vv. 20-21. This is the final cry of jubilation that concludes this series of prophecies. God has acted in anticipation, so declares his praise. As the exiles go out from Babylon, again an anticipated act, they are to declare Yahweh's redeeming action "*and* that they did not thirst. . . ." in the first exodus; Yahweh's actions now and in the past are joined; Israel now and in the past is one.

Verse 22, which is repeated virtually word for word in 57:21, has no relation to the context and seems to function as a divider for chaps. 40-66.

49:1-6, 7.
THE SECOND SERVANT SONG

49 Listen to me, O coastlands,
and hearken, you peoples from afar.
The LORD has called me from the womb,
from the body of my mother he named my name.
[2]He made my mouth like a sharp sword,
in the shadow of his hand he hid me;
he made me a polished arrow,
in his quiver he hid me away.
[3]And he said to me, "You are my servant,
Israel, in whom I will be glorified."
[4]But I said, "I have labored in vain,
I have spent my strength for nothing and vanity;
yet surely my right is with the LORD,
and my recompense with my God."

[5]And now the LORD says,
who formed me from the womb to be his servant,
to bring Jacob back to him,
and that Israel might be gathered to him,
for I am honored in the eyes of the LORD,
And my God has become my strength —
[6]he says:
"It is too light a thing that you should be my servant
to raise up the tribes of Jacob
and to restore the preserved of Israel;
I will give you as a light to the nations,
that my salvation may reach to the end of the earth."

[7]Thus says the LORD,
the Redeemer of Israel and his Holy One,
to one deeply despised, abhorred by the nations,
the servant of rulers:
"Kings shall see and arise;
princes, and they shall prostrate themselves;
because of the LORD, who is faithful,
the Holy One of Israel, who has chosen you."

This passage is the second of those commonly known as the servant songs. There is a break at the end of chap. 48. True, chaps. 49-55 make no mention of Cyrus, have no appeals to former prophecies, no polemics against idols, and prefer Zion-Israel to Jacob-Israel. But the great themes of election, call, salvation by Yahweh and servant are all there, as are the same rhetorical devices.

The literary form is a prophetic confession and call, *cf.*, Jer 1:4-10. The prophet, the individual, is speaking. But he is one with Israel (see 42:1-4) by which title Yahweh addresses him in v. 3 (see Excursus 2). Claus Westermann has pointed out that the passage is built around three sentences:

1a Listen to me, you coastlands....
5a Thus says Yahweh....
6b I make you a light to the nations....

The servant has been chosen and equipped for the task, vv. 1b-3; he has become discouraged, "But I...," v. 4; and now he is reassured, "But now Yahweh...," vv. 5-6.

vv. 1-2. The coastlands and nations are summoned, as in 41:1, though not to court. The call of the servant envisages the gentiles, as in 42:1-4. The servant is to fight with the word which penetrates like a sharp sword and at the same time reaches far and hits its mark like a well polished arrow. The great passage describing the effectiveness of God's word is 55:10-11, and the New Testament recalls that "the word of God is living and active, sharper than any two-edged sword, piercing to the division of soul and spirit, of joints and marrow, and discerning the thoughts and intentions of the heart," Heb 4:12. Part of the equipment is God's protecting hand, v. 2a, in the same sense as "hide me in the shadow of thy wings," Ps 17(16):8; "he will hide me in his shelter in the day of trouble," Ps 27(26):5; *cf.,* Ps 64(63):2-3, and his quiver in v. 2b which is in parallelism with "in the shadow of his hand."

v. 3. The servant now reports Yahweh's words to him which are best rendered: "You are my servant, you Israel in whom I take pride." Many authors want to climinatc "Israel" as a later addition. But an addition to what by whom? There is as good as no textual support for the omission, only one late 14th century Hebrew manuscript of not particularly good standing. "Israel" is found in the two Isaiah manuscripts from Qumran on the Dead Sea from the 1st or 2nd centuries B.C., and in the Greek Septuagint from the 3rd century B.C. The argument for omission on metrical grounds is quite unconvincing, while that from style and usage cannot stand. One has the impression that those who omit "Israel" from v. 3 have already decided that the servant is an individual and are really arguing in a circle — the servant is an individual, therefore Israel must fall from the text, which is the very point to be demonstrated with the text intact and in the context of chaps. 40-55.

The phrase, "you are my servant," *'abdi 'attah*, has been addressed to Israel already in 44:21. Israel and servant are in parallelism in 44:1, 21; 45:4. That Israel-Jacob-Jeshurun is the servant, my servant, is already familiar to one reading or hearing Second Isaiah, 41:8, 42:4; 43:10; 44:1-2; 44:21, 23; 45:4; 48:20 — all passages well set within Second Isaiah units. So when the reader arrives at 49:3 it is no surprise that the servant is identified fully as Israel. The view that Israel should be omitted from v. 3 is based solely on the hypothesis that the servant songs form a group of units independent of the body of chaps. 40-55, are the separate work of Second Isaiah or another, and have been inserted later into the complex; Israel was then added to bring the passage into line with what was already there. It is this last proposal that we reject emphatically.

v. 4. The servant protests, "but I, I said...," like Isa 6:5; Jer 1:6. The work so far has been futile, but his cause and his reward are with Yahweh, his God.

vv. 5-6. These verses have raised many difficulties and, because they seem to require that the servant, Israel, has a mission to Israel, have been used as an argument for the individual interpretation of the servant, because Israel could hardly have a mission to itself. This of course could be countered by pointing out that part of the mission of the Church is to the Church. Yahweh speaks, taking up the words of the servant in v. 1b. The infinitives, "to bring back" in v. 5a, "to raise up" in v. 6a, "to restore" in v. 6b, can have as their subjects either the servant or Yahweh; with the servant as subject the rendering is much as given in the RSV; with Yahweh as subject we read: "But now Yahweh, who formed me from the womb to be his servant, said, in his bringing back Jacob and gathering Israel to himself so that I have been honoured in the eyes of Yahweh and my God was my strength — and he said, it is a small thing for you to be my servant in my raising up the tribes of Jacob and my restoring the survivors of Israel, and so I make you my light to the gentiles, my salvation to the ends of the earth." This is to be preferred, despite some awkward syntax. Throughout chaps. 40-55 it is always Yahweh who is responsible for the acts which restore Israel, and if he uses an instrument, it is Cyrus, 44:28; 45:2f, 13; 46:10f; 48:14f. In the present passage it is again Yahweh in act. The sentences as rendered are somewhat prolix and syntactically loose, and a little longer than is usual for Second Isaiah. Verse 5c, "for I am honoured...," has struck many commentators as being out of place; hence it is often transferred so as to follow immediately on v. 3 or v. 4. But there is no manuscript evidence for this. So let the rendering proposed in this paragraph stand.

The part played by Israel, Yahweh's servant, in the restoration of the people is but small; not so its part as "my light (possessive pronoun from the parallel 'my salvation') to the gentiles and my salvation to the ends of the earth."

v. 7. This verse stands in a similar relation to vv. 1-6 as do

42:1-4. It is a further explanation of or application to vv. 1-6: Israel is "despised, abhorred. . . . the servant of rulers," *cf.*, 53:3. The contrast of despondency and sudden change is there in both, v. 4 and v. 7b, c, as so often in chaps. 50-55. Some commentators would have v. 7a, down to "servant of rulers," be followed directly by v. 8, minus "thus says the Lord," and transpose v. 7b, c, "kings shall see. . . ," so as to follow v. 12. But we have in v. 7 once again the basic relationship of the "redeemer and holy one" to the downtrodden Israel who shows himself faithful by his action, v. 7d.

49:8-26.
THE GLORIOUS RETURN
"THAT ALL MAY KNOW. . . ."

[8]Thus says the LORD:
"In a time of favor I have answered you,
in a day of salvation I have helped you;
I have kept you and given you
as a covenant to the people,
to establish the land,
to apportion the desolate heritages;
[9]saying to the prisoners, 'Come forth,'
to those who are in darkness, 'Appear.'
They shall feed along the ways,
on all bare heights shall be their pasture;
[10]they shall not hunger or thirst,
neither scorching wind nor sun shall smite them,
for he who has pity on them will lead them,
and by springs of water will guide them.
[11]And I will make all my mountains a way,
and my highways shall be raised up.
[12]Lo, these shall come from afar,
and lo, these from the north and from the west,
and these from the land of Syene."
[13]Sing for joy, O heavens, and exult, O earth;
break forth, O mountains, into singing!

For the LORD has comforted his people,
and will have compassion on his afflicted.

[14]But Zion said, "The LORD has forsaken me,
my Lord has forgotten me."

[15]"Can a woman forget her sucking child,
that she should have no compassion on the son of her womb?"
Even these may forget,
yet I will not forget you.
[16]Behold, I have graven you on the palms of my hands;
your walls are continually before me.
[17]Your builders outstrip your destroyers,
and those who laid you waste go forth from you.
[18]Lift up your eyes round about and see;
they all gather, they come to you.
As I live, says the LORD,
you shall put them all on as an ornament,
you shall bind them on as a bride does.
[19]"Surely your waste and your desolate places
and your devastated land —
surely now you will be too narrow for your inhabitants,
and those who swallowed you up will be far away.
[20]The children born in the time of your bereavement
will yet say in your ears:
The place is too narrow for me;
make room for me to dwell in.
[21]Then you will say in your heart:
'Who has borne me these?
I was bereaved and barren,
exiled and put away,
but who has brought up these?
Behold, I was left alone;
whence then have these come?"

[22]Thus says the LORD GOD:
"Behold, I will lift up my hand to the nations,
and raise my signal to the peoples;

and they shall bring your sons in their bosom,
and your daughters shall be carried on their shoulders.
[23]Kings shall be your foster fathers,
and their queens your nursing mothers.
With their faces to the ground they shall bow down to you,
and lick the dust of your feet.
Then you will know that I am the LORD;
those who wait for me shall not be put to shame."
[24]Can the prey be taken from the mighty,
or the captives of a tyrant be rescued?
[25]Surely, thus says the LORD:
"Even the captives of the mighty shall be taken,
and the prey of the tyrant be rescued,
for I will contend with those who contend with you,
and I will save your children.
[26]I will make your oppressors eat their own flesh,
and they shall be drunk with their own blood as with wine.
Then all flesh shall know
that I am the LORD your Saviour,
and your Redeemer, the Mighty One of Jacob."

49.8-26. Yahweh gives assurance of his favour and grace, of his liberating action, but Zion and its people are still plunged in gloomy despair. Their objections cannot stand because it is *he* who acts. With v. 14 begins a series of Zion poems, Zion being mentioned explicitly in 49:14; 51:3, 11, 16; 52:1-2, 7-8, and implicitly elsewhere. The general theme is the restoration of Jerusalem and its inhabitants by the action of Yahweh alone that "you may know," v. 23b, "all flesh may know," v. 26b, "that I am Yahweh. . . ." The prophet speaks in hyperbole and with a poetic *élan*, especially in vv. 19-21, which should not stand between the reader and the reality so well expressed centuries later by Paul: ". . . . where sin increased, grace abounded all the more . . . ," Rom 5:20. It is all the work of Yahweh. Verses 8-26 have been divided by many authors into two or three oracles. They are taken here as a unity, moving to the goal twice expressed in vv. 23b and 26b.

vv. 8-9a. The first words are taken up by Paul in 2 Cor 6:2 in the same sense — the era of salvation has come. The verbs in the perfect in v. 8a express the certainty of the salvation to come. v. 8a should be rendered: "I make you an assurance (pledge) to the people(s) in my raising up (restoring) the land and in my causing you to inherit your abandoned heritage." Yahweh is the initiator and agent throughout. v. 8b recalls 42:6 (see comment), *lit.*, "covenant of people," and v. 9a recalls 42:7.

vv. 9b-12. This is a description of the way home under God's protecting hand. The background and imagery are the first exodus and Ps 23(22), and there are echoes of 40:3-5 in v. 11. The passage moves to a climax in v. 12 — all the dispersed shall return, even those as far south as Aswan (Syene: this is Ezekiel's *s^{e}weneh* 29:10; 30:6, the *swn* of the Elephantine papyri, now attested in the Dead Sea Scroll of Isaiah; it is an ancient Jewish colony in south Egypt settled before 525 B.C.).

v. 13. One of several outbursts of joy in response to Yahweh's action, *cf.*, 44:23; 52:9. The whole of creation is involved and responds to God who saves.

vv. 14-21. Zion's lack of faith expresses itself in the language of a typical lament. Yahweh replies with one of the Bible's great expressions of the love of Yahweh for his people, which is better rendered: "Can a woman forget her sucking child, one pregnant (OR a compassionate mother) the child of her womb?" Zion is as it were engraved on Yahweh's hands and is ever present to him. The procession to Zion, v. 12, is referred to again in v. 18a in words taken up verbatim in 60:4. The restoration in population and territory staggers belief. The effect is heightened by the threefold repetition of "these" in v. 21.

vv. 22-23. Yahweh has only to raise his hand, give his signal, and the return shall begin. The kings who now rule his people will be subservient to them and lick the dust at their feet, *i.e.,* prostrate themselves before them in typical oriental fashion as illustrated in *ANEP*, no. 355, where Jehu is portrayed at the feet of Shalmeneser III. The purpose however is not that Zion be the proud ruler in their stead, but that she know with all her being that "I am Yahweh."

vv. 24-26. But pusillanimous Zion still doubts! She and her inhabitants to be must give a real assent to what Yahweh can accomplish. Verse 26a shocks us, but recalls events with which Israel and her neighbours were familiar, Deut 28:53-57; 2 Kgs 6:24-31. Again Yahweh points to the goal of his action, that "all flesh (humankind 40:5) shall know. . . ." The author resumes here an ancient title for God, "the Mighty One of Jacob," *'abîr Jacob*, found in Gen 49:24, and this whole half-verse is repeated verbatim in 60:16. In the words of C. R. North, the section ends "on a theocentric and universalist note."

50:1-3.
"I DIVORCED YOU? NO! IT'S YOUR FLAGRANT DISOBEDIENCE!"

50 Thus says the LORD:
"Where is your mother's bill of divorce,
with which I put her away?
Or which of my creditors is it
to whom I have sold you?
Behold, for your iniquities you were sold,
and for your transgressions your mother was put away.
2Why, when I came, was there no man?
When I called, was there no one to answer?
Is my hand shortened, that it cannot redeem?
Or have I no power to deliver?
Behold, by my rebuke I dry up the sea,
I make the rivers a desert;
their fish stink for lack of water,
and die of thirst.
3I clothe the heavens with blackness,
and make sackcloth their covering."

vv. 1-3. Yahweh, it seems, has been accused of divorcing his spouse, Israel, and of selling her to a creditor. He steps forward to answer the charges. "Where is the bill of divorce? who is the creditor?" v. 1b. The mother is Zion, those addressed are the children of Zion past and present. The questions are rhetorical and imply the answer, "No, they are non-existent!" When a husband divorces his wife he must give her a bill of divorce, Deut 24:1-4; Jer 3:8, 14; if she marries again, she cannot return to her former husband. A man may be forced to sell his children for debts incurred, Exod 21:7; 2 Kgs 4:1; Neh 5:5; Mt 18:25; he cannot insist on their return. Yes, Yahweh has sent his spouse away, but without the bill; he has sold his children, but not irrevocably. It is because of their own iniquity and flagrant disobedience that they have suffered. Verse 2a refers more likely to a continuation of Yahweh's defence, namely that there was no one at the tribunal to substantiate the accusation of abandonment, rather than to the frustrating work of the prophet to whom no one listened. Verses 2b-3 refer to Yahweh in his capacities as creator, ruler of the universe and redeemer; mythological and historical features are combined. Surely nothing, even restoration from the present parlous state of Zion, is beyond the lord of the universe. Verse 3 — it is he who lords the eclipses and controls the darkening sandstorms of the desert.

James Muilenburg argues strongly for the unity of the whole of chap. 50 on rhetorical grounds:

v. 1a, b	questions
c	behold!
v. 2a, b	questions
c	behold!
v. 8a, b	questions
v. 9	behold!
v. 10a, b	questions
v. 11	behold.

Then there is the repeated "Lord God," *'adonai Yahweh,* in vv. 4, 5, 7, 9.

50:4-9, 10-11. THE THIRD SERVANT SONG: RESPONSE

[4]The LORD GOD has given me
the tongue of those who are taught,
that I may know how to sustain with a word
him that is weary.
Morning by morning he wakens,
he wakens my ear
to hear as those who are taught.
[5]The LORD GOD has opened my ear,
and I was not rebellious,
I turned not backward.
[6]I gave my back to the smiters,
and my cheeks to those who pulled out the beard;
I hid not my face
from shame and spitting.

[7]For the LORD GOD helps me;
therefore I have not been confounded;
therefore I have set my face like a flint,
and I know that I shall not be put to shame;
[8]he who vindicates me is near.
Who will contend with Me?
Let us stand up together.
Who is my adversary?
Let him come near to me.
[9]Behold, the LORD GOD helps me;
who will declare me guilty?
Behold, all of them will wear out like a garment;
the moth will eat them up.
[10]Who among you fears the LORD
and obeys the voice of his servant,
who walks in darkness
and has no light,
yet trusts in the name of the LORD
and relies upon his God?
[11]Behold, all you who kindle a fire,
who set brands alight.

Walk by the light of your fire,
 and by the brands which you have kindled!
This shall you have from my hand:
 you shall lie down in torment.

Commonly known as the third servant song, vv. 4-9, with the response vv. 10-11, are a prophetic confession of one commissioned to convey the Lord's word. The prophet himself is speaking and his words can well reflect his own experience. Yahweh has called him, vv. 4-5a; despite opposition he has remained faithful and kept to his task. The "servant" is not mentioned in vv. 4-9, but is identified in v. 10. Once more it is the prophet at one with and standing over against his people (see Excursus 2).

vv. 4-9. The Lord Yahweh is the prime mover and is four times the subject of the verb(s): ". . . . has given me a disciple's tongue . . .," v. 4a, ". . . . has opened my ear . . .," 5a, ". . . . helps me . . .," vv. 7a, 9a. God has called the prophet to the office of the word and stays with him; the prophet in turn confesses his unshakeable confidence in God. The prophet is the disciple of Yahweh and his word and a witness to his faith. This is an exact description of prophecy in Israel — an event between God and his people (Claus Westermann).

vv. 4-5a. Verse 4 is best rendered:

The Lord Yahweh has given me a disciple's tongue
 that I may know how to sustain the weary:
with a word he stirs me in the morning,
 in the morning he stirs my ear to hear like a disciple.

The Lord called him to the office of the word. "But I, I did not resist . . .," v. 5b. He lived in faith the consequences of the call, v. 6. There can be no discouragement when the Lord God helps, v. 7. The language of vv. 8-9a is that of the law courts; the Lord God is his advocate; no one can accuse him of falling short in his office. The simile of v. 9a occurs again in 51:6, 8. The prophet is one with prophetic Israel.

vv. 10-11. The Lord addresses the Israelites and identifies the speaker of vv. 4-9 as the servant of Yahweh; v. 10 is interpreted:

> Who among you fears Yahweh, obeying the voice of
> his servant
> who walked in darkness with no light?
> Let him trust in Yahweh and take his stand on his God.

The address in v. 11 is to those Israelites who will not find their light in the servant's darkness, but kindle their own light. Their punishment from God, "my hand," however obscure, will be a bed of torment.

51:1-23 & 52:1-12.
THE RETURN TO ZION

> **51** "Hearken to me, you who pursue deliverance,
> you who seek the LORD;
> look to the rock from which you were hewn,
> and to the quarry from which you were digged.
> [2]Look to Abraham your father
> and to Sarah who bore you;
> for when he was but one I called him,
> and I blessed him and made him many.
> [3]For the LORD will comfort Zion:
> he will comfort all her waste places,
> and will make her wilderness like Eden,
> her desert like the garden of the LORD;
> joy and gladness will be found in her,
> thanksgiving and the voice of song.
>
> [4]"Listen to me, my people,
> and give ear to me, my nation;
> for a law will go forth from me,
> and my justice for a light to the peoples.
> [5]My deliverance draws near speedily,
> my salvation has gone forth,

and my arms will rule the peoples;
the coastlands wait for me,
and for my arm they hope.
[6]Lift up your eyes to the heavens,
and look at the earth beneath;
for the heavens will vanish like smoke,
the earth will wear out like a garment,
and they who dwell in it will die like gnats;
but my salvation will be for ever,
and my deliverance will never be ended.

[7]"Hearken to me, you who know righteousness,
the people in whose heart is my law;
fear not the reproach of men,
and be not dismayed at their revilings.
[8]For the moth will eat them up like a garment,
and the worm will eat them like wool;
but my deliverance will be for ever,
and my salvation to all generations."
[9]Awake, awake, put on strength,
O arm of the LORD;
awake, as in days of old,
the generations of long ago.
Was it not thou that didst cut Rahab in pieces,
that didst pierce the dragon?
[10]Was it not thou that didst dry up the sea,
the waters of the great deep;
that didst make the depths of the sea a way
for the redeemed to pass over?
[11]And the ransomed of the LORD shall return,
and come to Zion with singing;
everlasting joy shall be upon their heads;
they shall obtain joy and gladness,
and sorrow and sighing shall flee away.

[12]"I, I am he that comforts you;
who are you that you are afraid of man who dies,
of the son of man who is made like grass,
[13]and have forgotten the LORD, your Maker,

who stretched out the heavens
and laid the foundations of the earth,
and fear continually all the day
because of the fury of the oppressor,
when he sets himself to destroy?
And where is the fury of the oppressor?
[14]He who is bowed down shall speedily be released;
he shall not die and go down to the Pit,
neither shall his bread fail.
[15]For I am the LORD your GOD,
who stirs up the sea so that its waves roar —
the LORD of hosts is his name.
[16]And I have put my words in you mouth,
and hid you in the shadow of my hand,
stretching out the heavens
and laying the foundations of the earth,
and saying to Zion, 'You are my people.'"

[17]Rouse yourself, rouse yourself,
stand up, O Jerusalem,
you who have drunk at the hand of the LORD
the cup of his wrath,
who have drunk to the dregs
the bowl of staggering.
[18]There is none to guide her
among all the sons she has borne;
there is none to take her by the hand
among all the sons she has brought up.
[19]These two things have befallen you —
who will condole with you? —
devastation and destruction, famine and sword;
who will comfort you?
[20]Your sons have fainted,
they lie at the head of every street
like an antelope in a net;
they are full of the wrath of the LORD,
the rebuke of your God.

[21]Therefore hear this, you who are afflicted,
who are drunk, but not with wine:
[22]Thus says your Lord, the LORD,
your God who pleads the cause of his people:
"Behold, I have taken from your hand
the cup of staggering;
the bowl of my wrath
you shall drink no more;
[23]and I will put it into the hand of your tormentors,
who have said to you,
'Bow down, that we may pass over';
and you have made your back like the ground
and like the street for them to pass over."

52 Awake, awake,
put on your strength, O Zion;
put on your beautiful garments,
O Jerusalem, the holy city;
for there shall no more come into you
the uncircumcised and the unclean.
[2]Shake yourself from the dust, arise,
O captive Jerusalem;
loose the bonds from your neck,
O captive daughter of Zion.

[3]For thus says the LORD: "You were sold for nothing, and you shall be redeemed without money. [4]For thus says the Lord GOD: My people went down at the first into Egypt to sojourn there, and the Assyrian oppressed them for nothing. [5]Now therefore what have I here, says the LORD, seeing that my people are taken away for nothing? Their rulers wail, says the LORD, and continually all the day my name is despised. [6]Therefore my people shall know my name; therefore in that day they shall know that it is I who speak; here am I."

[7]How beautiful upon the mountains
are the feet of him who brings good tidings,
who publishes peace, who brings good tidings of good,

who publishes salvation,
who says to Zion, "Your God reigns."
[8]Hark, your watchmen lift up their voice,
together they sing for joy;
for eye to eye they see
the return of the LORD to Zion.
[9]Break forth together into singing,
you waste places of Jerusalem;
for the LORD has comforted his people,
he has redeemed Jerusalem.
[10]The LORD has bared his holy arm
before the eyes of all the nations;
and all the ends of the earth shall see
the salvation of our God.

[11]Depart, depart, go out thence,
touch no unclean thing;
go out from the midst of her, purify yourselves,
you who bear the vessels of the LORD.
[12]For you shall not go out in haste,
and you shall not go in flight,
for the LORD will go before you,
and the God of Israel will be your rear guard.

51:1-23 & 52:1-12.

These two chapters fall readily and conveniently into ten parts and form what is known as the great Zion poem or the great call to Zion. It matters little in the long run whether they were composed as a literary unit or are the result of a synthesis of disparate pieces. There is a general harmony of theme and structure. Eight of the ten stanzas or strophes (in the broad sense) begin with rousing imperatives, some with a repetition of the same word, 51:9; 51:17; 52:1; 52:11; others with imperatives in parallelism, 51:1; 51:4; and seven end on the note of joy, comfort, assurance, 51:3; 51:6; 51:8; 51:11; 51:16; 52:10; 52:12. The general theme is Yahweh the creator-saviour who acts. The following presents a synoptic view:

51:1-3	Harken to me... look to the rock	joy and gladness will be found in her, thanksgiving and the voice of song.
51:4-6	Look to me... and give ear	my salvation will be for ever, my deliverance will never be ended
51:7-8	Hearken to me fear not	but my deliverance will be for ever my salvation to all generations.
51:9-11	Awake, awake... (*'uri*)	everlasting joy shall be upon their heads...joy and gladness sorrow and sighing shall flee away.
51:12-16	I, I am he that comforts you	and saying to Zion, "you are my people."
51:17-20	Awaken yourself, awaken yourself (*hith'or*^{e}*ri*)	they are full of the wrath of of the Lord, the rebuke of your God.
51:21-22	Therefore, hear this	(they will pass over the backs of their tormentors)
52:1-6	Awake, awake... (*'uri*)	they shall know that it is I who speak here I am.
52:7-10	How beautiful on the mountains...	and all the ends of the earth shall see the salvation of our God.
52:11-12	Depart, depart...	for the Lord God will go before you, and the God of Israel will be your rear guard.

51:1-3, 4-6, 7-8. These three stanzas can be taken together. They have similar beginnings, "Hearken to me. . . ," "Listen to me. . . ," "Hearken to me. . . ," and each ends on a note of joy in the saving God. This does not necessarily mean that they were cast simultaneously from the same mould, though the evidence favours it. The leitmotif is "deliverance" or "saving action." The Hebrew *sedeq-sedaqah* (no difference in meaning) is rendered by "deliverance" in vv. 1a, 5a, 6c, 8b, and by "righteousness" in v. 7a. It is parallel to Yahweh himself in v. 1a, to "salvation" in vv. 5a, 6c, 8b, and to "*tôrāh*" in v. 7a. Both the overall context and the individual verses are predominantly salvific; hence the meaning of "saving action" must prevail over the (here) secondary meaning of devotion to the will and ordinances of God. If you are looking for Yahweh in his saving action, says v. 1, then look into your history. You are hewn from the quarry of Abraham and Sarah; they were one and old, and yet look how they were blessed and multiplied. How much more you! The author would be familiar with the many forms of the Eden motif, v. 3; *cf.,* Gen 2:8, 10, 15; 3:23, 24; 4:16; Ezek 28:13; 31:9; 31:16, 18. Here Eden is parallel to the garden of Yahweh, *cf.,* Ezek 28:13, 31:9. The language of vv. 4-5 is very much like that of the servant song in 42:1-4. A better rendering of v. 4b would be: "for my teaching (instruction) will go forth from me, and my law as a light to the peoples," understanding "my law" as explained under 42:4. The eternal Yahweh outlasts the "eternal" heavens and earth; they come to an end simply because they are not Yahweh, vv. 6b, 8b; ". . . . but you remain," *cf.,* Heb 1:11.

vv. 9-11. This section begins in the manner typical of a community lament; appeal is made to Yahweh's great deeds in the beginning and in history; the creator God is invoked as a warrior, "arm of the Lord." The same verb is used in the double imperative in 51:9, 17; 52:1. Four proper names are used for the primeval monster, Rahab, Tannin (dragon), Yam (sea), Tehom Rabbah (great deep); all are synonyms for the primeval chaos, for the state that was there before God drew cosmos out of chaos, *cf.,* Gen 1:2-3. The western,

Aristotelean idea of "nothing" was not part of the thought pattern of ancient Mesopotamia, Canaan and Israel; these people described "before creation" as the opposite of the order that they experienced in their universe — it was chaos, comprising darkness, the deep and the clashing of waters. The process towards order took the form of a struggle with the primeval monster and the imagery became part of Israel's cultural heritage transmitted from Mesopotamia through Canaan, constantly recurring in her poetry: Rahab, Isa 51:9; 30:7; Pss 87(86):4; 89(88):10; Job 9:12; 26:12; Tannin, Isa 51:9; 21:1; Jer 51:24; Ezek 29:3; 32:2; Job 7:12; Yam, Isa 51:9; Ps 74(73):13; Job 7:12; Hab 3:8. It is useful to compare Isa 27:1 with the mythological text from Ras Shamra, which reads:

> Crushed I not El's Belov'd Yamm?
> Destroyed I not El's Flood Rabbim?
> Did I not, pray, muzzle the Dragon?
> I did crush the crooked serpent,
> Shalyat (*šlyt*) the seven-headed.
>
> (*ANET*, 137, lines 35-38).

The proper name of the serpent is Lotan = Leviathan = the coiled or wriggly one (perhaps the evil one); *cf.*, Pss 74(73):14; 104(103):16; Job 41:1. The Isaiah text is: "In that day the Lord with his hand and great and strong sword will punish Leviathan the twisting (evil?) serpent, and he will slay the dragon that is in the sea," Isa 27:1. These are not examples of Israelite mythology but of the way in which Israel received and applied her cultural heritage and literary imagery. The creator God who triumphed over chaos and brought order into the world is the God who saves in history, v. 10bii. The last part of v. 11 could well consist of stock phrases and half lines such as are characteristic of the Homeric poems.

vv. 12-16. Yahweh the consoler speaks in response to vv. 9-11 — "I, I am he." How is it that Israel can possibly fear mortal human beings, made like grass, Ps 90(89):5; Isa 40:6, when her God is the creator God: men and women die, Yahweh is for ever, vv. 6, 7-8. The creator theme forms a literary inclusion in this passage, vv. 13 and 16, while the theme of Israel's humiliation and servitude alternates with that of Yahweh's power. That Israel is his servant is echoed in the words from the servant songs in v. 16a, *cf.*, 49:2; 50:4. The creator is the maker of the covenant who will restore his people precisely as the covenant people, v. 16c. The restoration is a new creation.

vv. 17-23. The prophet calls to Jerusalem to rouse herself from her hopelessness and be ready to receive Yahweh's oracle of promise, vv. 22-23. She is to rise from her drunken state induced by the cup of the divine wrath, a familiar image in the Bible: "Take from my hand this cup of the wine of wrath, and make all the nations to whom I send you drink it. They shall drink and stagger and be crazed because of the sword which I am sending among them," Jer 25:15-16, 17; *cf.*, Ezek 32:31-34; Lam 4:21; Ps 75(74):8. Israel has suffered and has deserved to suffer; Jerusalem-Judah has been destroyed and the population depleted, vv. 19-20. She has suffered "at the hand of the Lord," v. 17b, and because of "the wrath of the Lord. . . .the rebuke of your God," v. 20b, a literary inclusion underscoring the divine action. But despite her wretched state which Yahweh has brought about, he is on her side, "your God who pleads the cause of his people," v. 22. The roles are to be reversed and Israel's captors are to suffer her fate. In typical oriental fashion, and this is attested on bas-reliefs of ancient Near Eastern countries, Israel will walk over her erstwhile tormentors as they lie supine on the ground, *cf.*, Jos 10:24; Zech 10:5.

52:1-2, 3-6. In this rousing call to Zion-Jerusalem the prophet resumes the double imperatives of 51:9, 17, and addresses the city and exiles as one. There are eight imperatives in vv. 1-2; v. 2a should read: "shake yourself from the dust, rise up, be seated, Jerusalem!" The captive daughter of Zion is roused from the degradation and prostration of vv. 17-23 and is to be enthroned in vesture of honour. Verses 3-6 are in prose; they are probably less an interpolation than a call to the exiles to remember their history. ". . . for nothing. . . . without money": Yahweh is beholden to no one, but yet he is not arbitrary. He gains nothing from their exile, nothing from their return. Verse 5b remains obscure. The sojourn in Egypt, the exile of the northern kingdom and the capture of Jerusalem culminate in Yahweh's act of restoration — the people shall know that it is he who acts.

52:7-10, 11-12. This is a brilliantly imaginative portrayal of the bringing of the good news of liberation to the city of Zion. The poet pictures the messenger completing the 500 miles across the desert from Babylon and appearing over the crest of the mount of Olives — "as the mountains are round about Jerusalem," Ps 125(124):2. "Your God reigns" he cries in sight of the city. The watchmen take up the cry; they see at once that the return of the people is the return of Yahweh to Zion. It is difficult to convey the staccato intensity of the Hebrew: "How welcome upon the mountains the runner who proclaims, announces peace, proclaims good news, announces salvation, says to Zion, 'Your God reigns!' " v. 7. The singer, exultant, breaks into two imperatives: "Burst forth! shout with joy. . . . !" — even the ruins of the city are summoned to join in. The event is spoken of as already having happened — "(he). . . . has comforted — has redeemed — has bared. . . ," though this is but a proclamation. It is God's saving action (salvation), vv. 7b, 10b.

Another three imperatives in v. 11, the natural sequence to what has gone before, call on the exiles to leave Babylon as it were in a solemn liturgical procession with all due rites of purification performed. The final scene, v. 12, is best rendered emphatically:

> You shall not go out in haste,
> you shall not go in flight,
> Yahweh will go before you
> the God of Israel be your rear guard.

The constant exodus traditions are resumed, "Yahweh went before them by day in a pillar of cloud," Exod 13:21; Num

14:13; Deut 1:30-33; Ps 78(77):14; 1 Cor 10:1, and "the angel of God. . . . went behind them," Exod 14:19. The events proclaimed in 40:1-11 are now proclaimed as fulfilled.

52:13 — 53:12. THE SUFFERING SERVANT

[13]Behold, my servant shall prosper,
he shall be exalted, lifted up, on high,
[14]though many indeed were appalled at him.
Truly his countenance was disfigured by men,
his form by the sons of men.
[15]Truly he startled many nations,
before him kings shut their mouths,
for they saw what had not been told to them,
and they pondered what they had never heard.

53 Who has believed what we have heard,
and the arm (power) of Yahweh — upon whom
has it been bared (revealed)?
[2]Yet he shot up like a sapling before him,
like a root from arid ground.
No form was his nor beauty that we should look on him,
nor his countenance that we should desire him.
[3]Despised and most stupid of men,
a man of sufferings and experienced in illness,
and since he turned his face from us,
we considered him despised and a nothing.

[4]Truly it was he who bore our illness,
who carried our sufferings,
while we considered him stricken,
struck by God and afflicted.
[5]But he it was who was pierced by our rebellion,
crushed by our iniquities.
The punishment which brought our peace was upon
him,
and because of his wounds we are healed.

[6]We all have strayed like sheep,
each has followed his own way,
while Yahweh made fall on him the guilt of us all.

[7]Harshly used he submitted humbly
and did not open his mouth;
like a lamb he was led to the slaughter,
like a ewe before its shearers.
He was silent and did not open his mouth.
[8]From the custody of the court he was taken away,
and for his life, who gave a thought?
For he was cut off from the land of the living
and because of the rebellion of his people he was struck on their behalf.
[9]His grave was put with the wicked,
with the rich his burial mound,
though he had done no violence,
nor was there deceit in his mouth.
[10]But it was Yahweh's purpose to crush and pierce him.[1]
in truth he made his life an offering for sin.
He will see his offspring, he will lengthen his days,
and the purpose of Yahweh shall prosper because of him.
[11]With the anguish of his soul he was sated,
he was soaked with his sweat.[2]

My servant, righteous, will bring righteousness to many,
for it was he who carried their iniquities.
[12]Therefore I will give him a share with the great
and with the powerful he shall divide spoil,
inasmuch as he gave himself over to death
and let himself be counted with the rebels.
Yet it was he who bore the sins of many,
and interceded for the rebels.

([1]OR, "But Yahweh took pleasure in his humiliated one,"
OR, "Yahweh was pleased to crush him with sickness."
[2]for alternative, see commentary.)

(translation by author)

The passage may be divided as follows:

52:13-15 Yahweh speaks: the fate of "my servant."

53:1-11a The servant's suffering and exaltation — a report and a confession.

53:1 An incredible story.

2-3 He was insignificant, despised, nothing.

4-6 A confession: we thought that he was justly struck by God, but in fact *he* was carrying *our* guilt.

7-9 He suffered, innocent, without a word, and was as one given over to death and the grave.

10-11a Yahweh, whose will this was, will exalt him.

53:11b-12a Yahweh speaks again: my servant shall be vindicated.

This fourth song is very different of interpretation, as the history of exegesis shows. The first question to be asked is not who is "my servant" of 52:13a and 53:11b, but what is the song or oracle or report all about. It is misguided literalness to look for a historical equivalent of every detail, just as it is to look for equivalents in every detail of Jesus' parables. Verses 2-9 are not a detailed account of what actually happened to the servant; one must stand back and see the passage as a whole and set it in the stream of biblical language and imagery. The sufferings of the innocent one are described in the traditional terms of illness and persecution as are those of the man in Ps 22(21). The individual psalms of lament and the laments of Job form the literary background. The whole is framed between two oracles of Yahweh, 52:13-15 and 53:11b-12.

52:13-15. What certain people say, 53:1-11a, is set within the framework of what Yahweh says, 52:13-15 and 53:11b-12. The opening words, "Behold, my servant. . .," hark back to the very same words in 42:1 where "my servant" is assigned a task. Contrary to human expectations, the humiliated servant is to be raised up and exalted and this change of fortune will astonish the nations and their leaders, *cf.,* Ps 2:10. The compact contrast between humiliation and exaltation in 52:13-15 is spelled out in 53:2-12.

53:1. The verse is a transition linking easily with 52:15 by means of "what we have heard" 53:1a, and "what they had never heard" 52:15b. It is not said who the 'we' are. The arm or power of Yahweh recurs often in these chapters, 40:10-11; 48:14; 51:5; 51:9; 52:10. The power is revealed in the weakness of the servant.

vv. 2-3. The servant was utterly insignificant, a shoot or a wild tuft in the dry desert; v. 2b takes up the language of 52:14b. In v. 3 the servant is one who has suffered and is familiar with illness, the standard description of the sufferer in the psalms: "scorned by men and despised by the people," Ps 22(21):6; "take away from me their scorn and contempt," Ps 119(118):22; "I am a man who has seen affliction," Lam 3:1; see also Ps 69(68). The participle 'despised' is placed at the beginning and the end of the verse, *cf.*, 49:7.

vv. 4-6. A confession now interrupts the report. There is the eight (or nine) times repeated contrast between him (he) and us (we). The speakers, like the friends of Job, looked on the servant as one justly punished by God, v. 4b. In fact, however, he was carrying the burden of "our illness....our sufferings....our rebellion....our iniquities." Verse 6 begins and ends with the emphatic "we all....us all." The suffering of the servant is due to sin. Matthew resumes v. 4a in his report in which Jesus spends an evening healing diseases and casting out evil spirits, Matt 8:17. The servant suffers; the speakers now realize that he is suffering even more than they are and because of them.

vv. 7-9. The report continues. This section opens and closes with the literary inclusion, "and did not open his mouth," v. 7aii, and "nor was there deceit in his mouth," v. 9bii. The images of the lamb led to the slaughter, Jer 11:19, and of the one who was silent and did not open his mouth, Ps 38(37):13, are part of traditional description. Many scholars think that the sentence "he was cut off (*gāzar*) from the land of the living," v. 8b, is a description of the death of the servant. Claus Westermann, for example, says that he "suffered v. 7, died v. 8, and was buried v. 9." But once again the language is that of the individual lament. In Ps 88(87): 4-6 the psalmist complains:

I am reckoned among those who go down to the Pit;
I am a man who has no strength,
like one forsaken among the dead,
like the slain that lie in the grave,
like those whom thou dost remember no more,
for they are cut off (*gāzar*) from they hand.
Thou hast put me in the depths of the Pit,
in the regions dark and deep.

And Lamentations read:

The waters closed over my head,
I said, "I am cut off" (*gāzar*)
Lam 3:54.

The language is hyperbole. The individual songs of lament are full of expressions that describe the petitioner as succumbing to death, the grave and Sheol. Verses 7-9 describe the fate of Israel in the language and imagery of the individual lament. The servant, Israel, suffered because Israel had continually revolted against God, v. 8bii.

vv. 10-11. Once again the text is very difficult, especially vv. 10a and 11a. The report is finished and attention turns to Yahweh in act. The servant is described as if he were an expiatory sacrifice, v. 10aii, as an *'asham*, a guilt-offering. Nevertheless he shall prosper, and the prosperity is described in the traditional language of posterity and long life. There is further reflection on the satiety of the sufferings, v. 11. This difficult half-verse, 11a, may also be rendered: "After his life's labour he will see (OR be drenched with) light (word supplied from the Dead Sea Scroll of Isaiah, 1QIsa) and be sated with knowledge (experience)," OR "after his terrible experience he will enjoy the fullness of life."

vv. 11b-12. Yahweh speaks again. The servant was God's instrument through whom he acted to bring salvation to the many; the sufferings that the servant, Israel, bore are the means by which Israel will be vindicated by Yahweh who will reward him. It is not said how, as the imagery of dividing the spoils is traditional, *cf.*, Isa 9:3; Ps 68(67):12-13. In these one and a half verses the servant who suffers is described in five ways: 1) he carried their iniquities, 2) he gave himself over to death (death and Sheol are in parallelism in Prov 5:5; 7:27; Song 8:6; Ps 89(88):48; to be given over to death or Sheol is a traditional expression for extreme distress), 3) he let himself be counted with the rebels, 4) he bore the sins of many, 5) he interceded for the rebels. The servant, Israel, carried the sins of Israel; under Yahweh he went through suffering to vindication.

How then is this fourth song to be interpreted? The servant signifies, is a symbol of, Israel in history and captive Israel. Israel will recognize herself in the persecuted, suffering, sick man, just as she had recognized herself in the words of Isaiah of the 8th century:

> Ah, sinful nation, a people laden with iniquity,
> ....
> The whole head is sick, and the whole heart faint.
> From the sole of the foot even to the head,
> there is no soundness in it,
> but bruises and sores and bleeding wounds;
> they are not pressed out, or bound up,
> or softened with oil.
>
> Isa 1:4-6.

In 52:13-15 Yahweh states the situation of the servant — utterly humiliated, the servant will be raised up to the amazement of the nations and their kings. Shattered and captive Israel will be restored, and who would have believed it, 53:1a? and who is this one over whom the power of Yahweh is seen in act, 53:1b? He is one who is a nothing and despicable. The report now breaks off for three verses of community confession — "we....him....he....us." Israel in exile, Israel in general, Israel in her pious ones now reflects. Israel has suffered for Israel who has sinned; the present state of humiliation is all because of us, present Israel one with Israel of history. The report continues in vv. 7-9. Israel's fate is described in the traditional imagery of the psalms, Jeremiah, Lamentations and Job. The servant Israel is presented as one dragged off from the court, cut off from the land of the living and given over to the grave. The servant Israel is like the dry bones in the valley which Yahweh summons to life, Ezek 37:1-14 (a passage which one does not interpret literally); she can be brought to life again by Yahweh alone, vv. 10b, 11b-12. Israel the servant died in its own rebellious children; Israel carried Israel's sins; the pious Israel interceded for Israel.

But surely the servant is a vicarious sufferer. The texts point inexorably in this direction. "He bore our illness, carried our sufferings, v. 4a; "he carried their iniquities.... he bore the sins of many...," vv. 11b, 12c. But the words *nása'* = carry and *sābal* = bear a heavy load mean simply that; the servant Israel has carried the heavy load of Israel's sins. And in vv. 5a-b, 6b it is as a consequence of Israel's sins that the servant suffers. The main problem is v. 10a, "in truth he (Yahweh) made his life an offering for sin (guilt-offering)"; the word is *'asham*. It means "an offense, and then the means by which the offence is righted, and, finally, a sacrifice of reparation" (R. de Vaux, *Ancient Israel*, p. 420). There is no entirely satisfactory explanation of the half-verse 10aii; one can only say rather limply that Yahweh regarded Israel's suffering, which he himself brought about, as some sort of offering for sin. And the protestations of innocence are best understood in the context of the protestations of the sufferers in the psalms. "My servant, righteous, will bring righteousness to many," v. 11b, does not look to the vicarious, expiatory sufferer, but to Israel, the servant, the one through whom Yahweh has seen fit to exercise his saving action, much as Noah was the chosen vessel through whom God exercised his saving action in the flood, Gen 6:9; 7:1. Both the servant and Noah were *saddīq*, "righteous," select instruments through whom God worked.

54:1-10.
RESTORATION BY THE GOD OF COMPASSION

54 "Sing, O barren one, who did not bear;
break forth into singing and cry aloud,
you who have not been in travail!
For the children of the desolate one will be more
than the children of her that is married, says the LORD.
[2]Enlarge the place of your tent,
and let the curtains of your habitations be stretched out;
hold not back, lengthen your cords
and strengthen your stakes.
[3]For you will spread abroad to the right and to the left,
and your descendants will possess the nations
and will people the desolate cities.

[4]"Fear not, for you will not be ashamed;
be not confounded, for you will not be put to shame;
for you will forget the shame of your youth,
and the reproach of your widowhood you will
remember no more.
[5]For your Maker is your husband,
the LORD of hosts is his name;
and the Holy One of Israel is your Redeemer,
the God of the whole earth he is called.
[6]For the LORD has called you
like a wife forsaken and grieved in spirit,
like a wife of youth when she is cast off,
says your God.
[7]For a brief moment I forsook you,
but with great compassion I will gather you.
[8]In overflowing wrath for a moment
I hid my face from you,
but with everlasting love I will have compassion on you,
says the LORD, your Redeemer.

[9]"For this is like the days of Noah to me:
as I swore that the waters of Noah
should no more go over the earth,

so I have sworn that I will not be angry with you
 and will not rebuke you.
[10]For the mountains may depart
 and the hills be removed,
but my steadfast love shall not depart from you,
 and my covenant of peace shall not be removed,
 says the LORD, who has compassion on you.

The passage portrays in emotive language the transition from lamentation to joy. There is complete change, a new state of salvation, all brought about by Yahweh himself. Zion is addressed, as the many feminine forms of nouns and verbs indicate, and many of the typical stylistic devices of Second Isaiah are there, imperatives and contrasts, the heaping up of titles applied to Yahweh in v. 5, and the repetition of the key words "steadfast love" and "compassion" in vv. 8-10.

vv. 1-3. In 42:23 and 49:13 the whole of creation is called to sing because of Yahweh's saving acts on Israel's behalf; here it is Israel herself that is called upon. The prophet takes up the familiar theme of lament and joy. Yahweh makes the barren and childless one a mother, as in Ps 113(112):9, a figure that was traditional in Israel — Sarah, Rachel, Hannah. The image of the tent recalls the patriarchal period with its blessings and promise of increase. Rejoicing at what is to come, the wife is to get to work at once and enlarge the tent to provide for the blessing of so many children.

vv. 4-8. In typical fashion the prophet heaps together a succession of nouns and verbs meaning shame and humiliation, v. 4, as well as the already familiar titles of Yahweh, v. 5. The marriage relationship between Israel and her God, apparently broken, will be restored in full. Verses 7-8 are the climax of the passage and are at the heart of the message of Second Isaiah, ending with the juxtaposition of eternal steadfast love and compassion, Yahweh and redeemer.

vv. 9-10. The prophet reaches back to an event in primeval time for his comparison. There is to be something new, as in Gen 8:21-22 and 9:11-17, and the assurance for the future is just as solemn. The speaker is Yahweh the compassionate: "Yahweh, Yahweh, a God merciful and gracious, slow to anger and abounding in steadfast love and faithfulness, keeping steadfast love for thousands, forgiving iniquity...," Exod 34:6-7. In the context of the creator-redeemer theology the prophet has Yahweh assert his permanent love (*hesed*) and his covenant of peace (*shālôm*). *Hesed* and *shālôm* together signify peace, welfare, well being, and recall the "new covenant," Jer 31:31; and Ezek 37:26: "I will make a covenant of peace with them; it shall be an everlasting covenant with them; and I will bless them and multiply them...." And when is all this to be fulfilled? the "promise of an interrupted condition of salvation points far beyond history, or far beyond the path trodden by God's people on their journey through history" (C. Westermann).

54:11-17.
THE NEW JERUSALEM

[11]"O afflicted one, storm-tossed, and not comforted,
behold, I will set your stones in antimony,
and lay your foundations with sapphires.
[12]I will make your pinnacles of agate,
your gates of carbuncles,
and all your wall of precious stones.
[13]All your sons shall be taught by the LORD,
and great shall be the prosperity of your sons.
[14]In righteousness you shall be established;
you shall be far from oppression, for you shall not fear;
and from terror, for it shall not come near you.
[15]If any one stirs up strife,
it is not from me;
whoever stirs up strife with you
shall fall because of you.
[16]Behold, I have created the smith
who blows the fire of coals,

and produces a weapon for its purpose.
I have also created the ravager to destroy;

[17]no weapon that is fashioned against you shall prosper,
and you shall confute every tongue that rises against you in judgment.
This is the heritage of the servants of the LORD
and their vindication from me, says the LORD."

The speaker throughout is Yahweh who describes in flashing imagery the glory of the new Jerusalem with the background theme of the forsaken wife and assures her that his saving action is her foundation and will protect her from all harm. The beginning is rather abrupt, but the ending is the traditional formula, "oracle of Yahweh."

vv. 11-13. The motif of precious stones is found in Ezek 28:13. The point here is that the new Jerusalem will be Yahweh's work, and hence full of brilliance. The theme is resumed in Rev 21:19-21. The word rendered "antimony" is probably the modern eye-shadow with which Jezebel painted herself, 2 Kgs 9:30. "Pinnacles" derives from the Hebrew word for the sun, *shemesh*, and continues the picture of flashing brilliance, and "carbuncles" contains the root for striking a fire — "glowing stones." Following the first Isaiah scroll from the Dead Sea we may read "all your workers" for "all your sons" at the beginning of v. 13; Yahweh directs the rebuilding of the new Jerusalem.

vv. 14-17. Yahweh now assures Jerusalem that "you shall be established in righteousness"; better, you are being set up or restored by his saving action, a promise made in the context of "welfare," *shālôm*, in v. 13b. There are mingled in these verses both a promise of blessing and a promise of salvation which are to introduce a new era. Any attacks on Zion must fail, vv. 14b-15. Why? because Yahweh it is who created (*bārā'*, used twice in v. 16) both the forgers of weapons and those who seek to destroy. All is summed up in v. 17b — "their vindication (*sedaqah, i.e.,* salvation) is from me"; that is, the citizens of Jerusalem are to enjoy the benefits of Yahweh's saving action.

55:1-13.
THE EVERLASTING COVENANT

55 "Ho, every one who thirst,
come to the waters;
and he who has no money,
come, buy and eat!
Come, buy wine and milk
without money and without price.
[2]Why do you spend your money for that which is not bread,
and your labor for that which does not satisfy?
Hearken diligently to me, and eat what is good,
and delight yourselves in fatness.
[3]Incline your ear, and come to me;
hear, that your soul may live;
and I will make with you an everlasting covenant,
my steadfast, sure love for David.
[4]Behold, I made him a witness to the peoples,
a leader and commander for the peoples.
[5]Behold, you shall call nations that you know not,
and nations that knew you not shall run to you,
because of the LORD your God, and of the Holy One of
Israel,
for he has glorified you.

[6]"Seek the LORD while he may be found,
call upon him while he is near;
[7]let the wicked forsake his way,
and the unrighteous man his thoughts;
let him return to the LORD, that he may have mercy on
him,
and to our God, for he will abundantly pardon.
[8]For my thoughts are not your thoughts,
neither are your ways my ways, says the LORD.
[9]For as the heavens are higher than the earth,
so are my ways higher than your ways
and my thoughts than your thoughts.

[10]"For as the rain and the snow come down from heaven,
and return not thither but water the earth,

making it bring forth and sprout.
giving seed to the sower and bread to the eater,
[11]so shall my word be that goes forth from my mouth;
it shall not return to me empty,
but it shall accomplish that which I purpose,
and prosper in the thing for which I sent it.

[12]"For you shall go out in joy,
and be led forth in peace;
the mountains and the hills before you
shall break forth into singing,
and all the trees of the field shall clap their hands.
[13]Instead of the thorn shall come up the cypress;
instead of the briar shall come up the myrtle;
and it shall be to the LORD for a memorial,
for an everlasting sign which shall not be cut off."

The prophet now brings his message to a conclusion evoking many of the themes sounded in the opening passage, 40:1-11 — forgiveness, 40:2 and 55:6-7; return, 40:3-5 and 55:12-13; the participation of nature in the return, 40:4 and 55:12; the word and its enduring effect, 40:8 and 55:10-11. Yahweh, who is the speaker throughout, summons the exiles to leave Babylon and share in the life, spiritual and material, that he is offering them in their own land. He assures them that the covenant made with David has not been broken but transferred to the people. Stylistically there is the typical Second Isaian use of imperatives, vv. 1-2a, 2b-3a, 6.

vv. 1-5. One must, I think, set the first two verses in the tradition of the call of Wisdom to eat and drink, as we read in Prov 9:5; Sir 24:19. Yahweh calls; there is to be no bargaining, no money is to change hands. He gives freely of his grace — water, a necessity of life; wine and milk, the symbols of abundance. The imagery of hunger and thirst is often used to express spiritual realities: Prov 9:5-6; Pss 42(41):2; 63(62):1; 143(142):6; John 4:10ff; 7:37-38. But we must be careful not to make a fast distinction between

Yahweh's spiritual and material benefits; Israel saw them as one, coming from the source of all blessing. Verse 2a, "that which is not bread," may refer to life in Babylon, while the "good" (the grain?) and the "fatness" (the oil?) of v. 2b cover all the produce of the earth and the cattle industry. A number of authors, while not excluding the reference to Wisdom, understand the call of v. 1 from the background of the water-carriers in the Middle East who sell their precious commodity in the streets and market places — even today (they have served my needs in many cities, towns and villages in the area). But I wonder if this is not reading back into Babylon one of the more unusual and attractive features of Middle Eastern life which caught the attention of the European when he discovered life there in the 19th and 20th centuries. In v. 3a, rather than "that your soul may live," a better rendering would be "that you may have the fullness of life."

The fullness of life is now expressed in terms of the covenant: "I will make a lasting covenant with you (which will consist in my) enduring acts of steadfast love to David," v. 3b. The lasting (not an abstract, metaphysical notion of endless time) covenant is mentioned in Isa 24:5; 61:8; it is that given to David, 2 Sam 7:8-16; 23:5; 1 Kgs 8:23-26; Ps 89(88):19-37. Yahweh is saying that the covenant made with David and the promises have not been broken, despite the end of the monarchy in Jerusalem, but have now been transferred to the people. David had been a witness, leader and commander to the peoples, ". . . . you made me the head of the nations; people whom I have not known served me," Ps 18(17):43. But now it is Israel who shall call nations she does not know, and nations who do not know her shall run to her, v. 5a, and it is Israel who is to be Yahweh's witness, *cf.*, Isa 43:10; 44:8. The destiny of Israel "my servant" is not to conquer and subdue nations, but to witness to Yahweh; she will increase not by conquest but by witness which will draw people to her. And all this is done by Yahweh for the glorification of Israel.

vv. 6-11. The words of Second Isaiah come to a conclusion. One sought the Lord originally in a cultic setting; one went to a sanctuary. Here the meaning is, "turn to God now! at this very moment of deliverance from Babylon; repent now." It had all seemed so impossible; how could poor, helpless, captive Israel return in triumph from the power of Babylon? There are two reasons why she can return: 1) because of God's mysterious purpose, vv. 8-9; 2) because God has spoken and his word is event, vv. 10-11. Yahweh effects his will for Israel through the most unlikely instruments. The word "thoughts" in vv. 8-9 is best rendered "purpose" or "designs." God's purpose is a constant concern with Second Isaiah — 44:28; 46:10; 48:14; 53:10. Later, Paul was to burst into praise at the ways of God in another context: "O the depth of the riches and wisdom and knowledge of God! How unsearchable are his judgments and how inscrutable his ways!" Rom 11:33, and then went on to quote Isa 40:13-14. Second Isaiah's words in 55:8-9 are a general statement applied to the particular context of Babylon. So too are the following, vv. 10-11, about God's word.

God's word is not merely content; it is event. It is the instrument by which he effects his purpose. He has said through his prophet that Israel will leave Babylon, and this must come about "for the word of the Lord has spoken" and "the word of our God will stand for ever," Isa 40:5, 8; see further Isa 9:8; Jer 1:4; Pss 33(32):6; 147:15, 18; Wis 16:12; 18:14-16. The word of God must not be hypostasized in this context, nor must any magical power be attributed to it; it does not work automatically. It is always received by a person, but only if that person listens, attends. Nevertheless God achieves his purpose through his word. The rain and snow soak the earth and so give man and woman their food; so too God's word is effective. The Hebrew *dābār* means both word and event (*cf.*, comm. 40:8).

Second Isaiah speaks of the word and its effectiveness in the tradition of the ancient Near East from the Summerian *enem*, the voice of the god Enlil, to the Proverbs of Ahiqar in the 5th century, down to the Book of Wisdom, 18:14-15.

In the Aramaic Proverbs of Ahiqar, probably composed a century or so before the 5th century manuscript, we read:

> For a word is a bird;
> once released no man *can re*[*capture it*]
> (OR who releases it is a man of no *un*[*derstanding*])
> ....
> Soft is the utterance of a king;
> (yet) it is sharper and stronger than a [two]-edged knife
> ....
> Soft is the tongue of *a* [*king*],
> but it breaks a dragon's ribs (*cf.*, Prov 25:15).
> (*ANET*, 428-29).

vv. 12-13. Israel will leave Babylon, and nature will respond as in Pss 96(95):12-13; 98(97):8. The desert shall become a royal park; it will be as it were a lasting inscription which shall not be effaced. Creation and history are again seen as an inseparable unity. Second Isaiah began on a note of comfort; he ends on a note of joy.

The prophet of the exile was a forthteller, not a foreteller. That is, he proclaimed Yahweh's saving action of deliverance; he did not predict the details. The exiles straggled home in unpretentious groups and caravans; there was no highway through the desert, no miracle of nature. Yet they did go home, but to a destiny that they did not conceive. From the ruined city and Temple they were to rise not as political power, but as "a pledge to the peoples. . . . a light to the nations," assuring people and shining in their fidelity to the way of Yahweh.

Excursus 2. The Problem of the Servant Songs

When Bernhard Duhm (1892) detached chaps. 40-66 of the book of Isaiah from the prophet of the 8th century and assigned them, with good reasons, to the exilic or post-exilic periods, he also detached the servant songs (42:1-4; 49:1-6; 50:4-9; 52:13 - 53:12) from the prophet of the exile and assigned them to an unknown teacher of the law in the middle of the 5th century; they were inserted later into chaps. 40-55 he contended. In the following decades the great majority of exegetes followed Duhm inasmuch as they understood the songs as a separate strand running through the chapter composed and inserted later either by the prophet himself, a contemporary, a disciple or a later unknown hand. Some readily concede that the songs may well be the work of Second Isaiah (C. Westermann). In any case, it is maintained, the songs belong to a different category from the rest of the poems in chaps. 40-55, do not fit readily into their immediate context and hence are to be considered in themselves.

There had been many attempts to identify the servant before Duhm, particularly the servant of the fourth song: he was Hezekiah, Isaiah, Uzziah, Jeremiah, Second Isaiah, Zerubbabel, an anonymous saint or prophet. Since Duhn the following have been awarded the title: Eleazar (Maccabean period, 2 Macc 6:18-21), Jehoiachin, Zerubbabel, Moses, Ezekiel, Cyrus, a political messianic figure who was a contemporary of Second Isaiah. Other theories would combine several of these: 42:1-4, 5-8 and 49:1-6 describe King Hezekiah, 715(725?)-687, who also composed them; Jeremiah is the subject and author of 50:4-9, while 52:13 -53:12 was written by Isaiah of King Uzziah who was afflicted with leprosy; it was later heavily interpolated.

Ernst Sellin across a long and distinguished career proposed several candidates: Zerubbabel (1898), Jehoiachin (1901), Moses (1922), Second Isaiah (1930). Finally in 1937 he supported the view that the first three songs were autobiographical and were written by Second Isaiah, while the fourth was written by Trito-Isaiah (author of chaps. 56-66 and a creature of Duhm's) as an epilogue to the career of his martyred master Second Isaiah, the great prophet of the exile.

The autobiographical interpretation, more or less as accepted by Sellin, has received strong support from some Old Testament scholars. The late Karl Elliger was of the opinion that most of chaps. 40-55 were written by Second Isaiah who was put to death by the Babylonian authorities; these poems were collected by Trito-Isaiah who added the fourth song. J. Begrich, subscribing to the autobiographical view, considered the fourth song to have been written by Second Isaiah in anticipation of his own death. A contemporary scholar, R. N. Whybray (1978), maintains that the servant of Yahweh in chap. 53, as in the other servant songs, is the prophet whom we call Second Isaiah. He was arrested because of his anti-Babylonian prophecies, tried, convicted and imprisoned. As a consequence he lost all standing among his fellow exiles who now saw him either as a false prophet from the first or one from whom Yahweh had withdrawn his favour. They would have no more to do with him; he was as good as dead. But a miracle occurred; the prophet was either released or escaped from prison and appeared once more among the exiles.

The distinguished critic Karl Budde, writing at the turn of the century, was not impressed by the attempts to identify the servant and considered them as "nothing short of fantastic, and the extreme of absurdity."

At the same time there were many scholars who interpreted the servant songs in a collective sense as empirical Israel, ideal Israel, the pious remnant, the order of prophets, or combinations of these. A. S. Peake and H. Wheeler Robinson in England stressed the corporate personality aspect, and Otto Eissfeldt strongly supported the collective interpretation: the servant is Israel Eissfeldt wrote: he is "both identical with Israel and at the same time also not identical. He shares in the fate and guilt of empirical Israel and is yet at the same time, as a kind of ideal Israel, an example and saviour for the other nations and for empirical Israel itself. . . . Israel has had to bear its hard fate for the sake of a high purpose, namely that its God should be recognized and honoured in all the world as the only and true God, not only by all Israelites but by all the world."

Conservative opinion both in the Catholic and Reformed tradition has constantly favoured a messianic interpretation of the servant. Jewish tradition in the first thousand years of Christianity understood the messiah-servant as ben-David, son of David; since the Middle Ages a collective interpretation has prevailed, though some writers have proposed an individual interpretation.

The two main reasons given for separating the songs from the rest of chaps. 40-55 are: 1) their loose connection with the immediate context, 2) the difference between the statements about the servant in the songs and outside the songs. The first reason carries no weight because chaps. 40-55 are a collection of songs and many passages seem to have no connection with their immediate context. The second reason is not cogent because there are so many similarities between the language and phraseology of the songs and the other poems.

The servant is regularly identified with Israel outside the songs: 41:8-10; 43:10; 44:1-2; 44:21; 45:4; 48:20; 49:7; in 54:17 the "servants of the Lord" are God's loyal Israelites; in 42:19 the servant is Israel in exile. There are in all some fourteen instances where the servant is Israel. In the songs, however, the term servant describes an individual: "my servant" 42:1; 49:3, 6; "his servant" 49:5. The commentary on or elaboration of the third song refers to "his servant," 50:10, while the "Yahweh statements" of the fourth song speak of "my servant" 52:13; 53:11. The name Israel occurs but once in the songs, 49:3. But if the servant songs belong to chaps. 40-55 and are the work of the prophet then there is no option but to understand the servant as Israel. The servant of the songs speaks or is spoken of as an individual. But outside the songs he is also an individual: he is "thou," 42:8-16; he has a right hand, 41:13; he has eyes and ears but cannot see or hear, 42:19; he is formed by Yahweh from the womb, 44:1-2, as he is in the second song, 49:1. The servant-prophet speaks as one with his people, 49:1-6; 50:4-9, yet stands over against the people; the people, Israel, is the Israel of history, empirical Israel, faithless Israel, yet at the same time the true Israel which is to be God's instrument to redeem Israel; the servant-people is Israel with a mission to Israel; and the prophet is conscious that he is one with the people that has been hewn from Abraham, 51:1-2. When Israel suffers, she suffers for Israel and for the vindication of Israel by Yahweh (see comments on individual songs). The salvation of Israel by Yahweh the creator and redeemer is the theme of the whole of chaps. 40-55; Israel the people is the centre of the prophet's pronouncements.

Recent surveys of monographs (1980) and periodical literature (1978) on Second Isaiah note a striking and widespread tendency on the one hand to leave the servant songs as an integral part of chaps. 40-55, the work of the prophet; and on the other to turn away from the interpretation that sees the servant as Israel. Though scholars recognize the individual qualities of the servant, they hesitate to make a specific identification. The present commentary agrees that the songs belong to the whole and are a creation of Second Isaiah, but argues with James Muilenburg that ". . . . if the servant songs are the work of Second Isaiah and an integral part of his poetic compositions, then the servant of the Lord is certainly Israel," and that ". . . . the fact remains that no single person is sufficient to bear the burden of what is disclosed in the songs"; further that "Israel, and Israel alone, is able to bear all that is said about the servant of the Lord." The prophet-poet speaks about Israel under the form of an individual in what are called servant songs in which every detail is not to be pressed to the letter.

The Servant in the New Testament

The New Testament applies many passages from Second Isaiah, particularly from the servant songs, to Jesus. The synoptic and Johannine traditions see John the Baptist as "the voice crying. . . prepare the way of the Lord" — Mark 1:1-2; Matt 3:1-3; Luke 3:1-6; John 1:19-23; Isa 40:3. Jesus is "my beloved son; with thee I am well pleased," Mark 1:11 (with parallels); Isa 42:1; he is "the lamb of God who takes away the sin of the world," John 1:29; Isa 53:7, 12; "truly it was he who bore our illness," Matt 8:17; Isa 53:4. Matthew quotes the whole of the first servant song, Isa 42:1-4, in the context of Jesus' ministry, Matt 12:15-21. The theme of "my beloved son" occurs again in the Transfiguration scene Mark 9:2-8; Matt 17:1-8; Luke 9:28-36. Jesus came "to give his life as a ransom for many," Mark 10:45; Isa 53:10, 11b-12, and "he was reckoned with the transgressors," Luke 22:37; Isa 53:9. The theme of Israel's destiny to be "light to the nations," Isa 42:6; 49:6, is taken up by Simeon in the Temple, Luke 2:32. The theme "the Spirit of the Lord God is upon me. . . ." from a later part of Isaiah, 61:1-2, is applied by Jesus to himself in the synagogue at Capernaum, Luke 4:18-19; *cf.*, Luke 7:22. The gospel tradition identified Jesus with the second Israel, the true servant of Yahweh. It is not unreasonable to conclude that this identification had its origins in Jesus himself, though some would disagree. However it is one thing for the earliest Christian tradition to understand Jesus as the second Israel and the fulfilment of what is said of the servant in Second Isaiah, and to do this quite legitimately; it is another thing to read this back into the prophet of the exile and in particular to allow Jesus' suffering, death and resurrection to determine the exegesis of the fourth song.

Excursus 3. Sedeq-sedaqah *(righteousness, victory).*

The words *sedeq-sedaqah* (no notable difference in meaning) recur constantly in Second Isaiah, predominantly in a salvific sense. The following schema lists the texts, the translations by the RSV and the Jerusalem Bible, and some comments. For further details, see the explanations in the commentary.

Text	**RSV**	**JB**	**Comments**
41:2a	victory	victory	God's saving Cyrus
41:10b	my victorious right hand	my victorious right hand	God supports his people
42:6	in righteousness	to serve the cause of right	in (my) salvific purpose
42:21	for his righteousness' sake	for the sake of his integrity	because of his salvific purpose
45:8	righteousness	victory	God's saving action: 3 key words: *sedeq, yesh'a, sedaqah*
45:13	righteousness	victory	in (my) salvific purpose
45:19c	speak the truth	speak with directness	God is found in world order; his are one
45:23	in righteousness	in truth	due order that comes from God

45:24	righteousness	victory	plural of *sedaqah*, "saving acts"
45:25	shall triumph	shall be victorious	shall be prosperous: verb form from *sdq*
46:12-13	deliverance	victory	God's action in restoring his people
48:1	right	uprightness	with *'emet*, truth
48:18	righteousness	integrity	parallel with *shālôm*, prosperity
51:1,5,7	deliverance (2) righteousness	integrity (3)	parallel to Yahweh, salvation truth
51:6,7	deliverance (2)	integrity, salvation	parallel to *yeshu'ah*, saving power
54:14,17	righteousness vindication	integrity salvation	a promise to the afflicted in the context of *shālôm* v. 13b.

As a background to *sedeq-sedaqah*, "righteousness," in the context of salvific action and prosperity, it is useful to study such texts as Pss 72(71):1-3; 85(84):9-13; Isa 32:1-17, particularly vv. 16-17. Isaiah chap. 32 begins:

> Behold, a king will reign by righteousness,
> and princes will rule by justice.

Rulers who rule in this way will be

> like streams of water in a dry place,
> like the shade of a great rock in a weary land.

The similes represent material prosperity and well-being. Later in the chapter, vv. 9-14, there is a lament over a scene of desolation. This lasts until the Spirit is poured from on high, v. 15. Then the wilderness becomes a fruitful field and the fruitful field becomes a forest, and *mishpat*, "justice," dwells in the wilderness and *sedaqah*, "righteousness," in the fruitful field. And the effect of *sedaqah* will be *shālôm*, prosperity, quietness and trust for ever, v. 17. God's saving action through his Spirit brings material prosperity and peace.

In Second Isaiah *sedeq-sedaqah* is constantly used for Yahweh's saving activity and its effects in the life of his covenant people. One of the most important of these effects is the peace, harmony and well-being of the community. *Sedeq-sedaqah* very often indicates prosperity. This fits in very well with the conclusion of H. H. Schmid in his detailed study of *sdq: "sdq* in Second Isaiah then means Yahweh's world order in salvation history, an order that is based on creation and extends over the proclamation of the divine will, the rousing of Cyrus and the 'servant' right up to the coming of the salvation of the future."

CHAPTERS 56-66

1. Historical Background to Chaps. 56-66

Our biblical sources of information for the period immediately following Cyrus' decree in 538 allowing the return from exile are Ezra 1-6 (omitting 4:6, 7-23), Haggai and Zechariah 1-8, all of whom are concerned with the years 521-515 when the Temple was being rebuilt.

Jerusalem-Judah was not made a province of the neo-Babylonian Empire in 587. Samaria, overthrown and possessed by the Assyrians in 722, was the province while Jerusalem-Judah remained a vassal under the supervision of the governor of Samaria, comprising scarcely more than the city of Jerusalem itself and its immediate environs. The northern border was the Bethel-Mizpah area no more than ten miles to the north, while the southern limit, though uncertain, may well have extended only the six miles to Bethlehem and Netopha, or perhaps to the line through Hebron and Beth-Zur, another ten miles to the south, the border during the Persian period. Under the administration of the governor of Samaria the lands were probably let out to the upper classes, the descendants of those brought to settle there under the Assyrians in the 8th century. There was then a ready made state of friction when the exiles returned. The text of Cyrus' decree permitting the rebuilding of the Temple is given in Ezra 1:1-4 (Hebrew); 6:2-5 (Aramaic). It is referred to in 2 Chron 36:22-23 in almost the same terms as in Ezra 1:1-4. This was in accordance with Cyrus' policy as we know from the cylinder inscription (*ANET*, 315-316). The Hebrew version of the decree gives permission to those who wish to go up to Jerusalem. It is not easy to say how many returned from Babylon. Some critics think that the first response to the decree was not great, others speak of thousands returning, while another is of the opinion that the first returns took place only in the reign of Cambyses, 528-522. At any rate these repatriates, the descendants of the deported property-owning upper classes, were, at least in their own minds, the legitimate heirs of much of the land. Provision had to be made for them, which did not please the descendants of the Assyrian transplants, the Samaritans, to whom the land had been let. Those who returned seem to have been rather poor and not particularly well organized. The Chronicler makes an immediate connection between the return of the first exiles and the building of the altar and the laying of the foundations of the second Temple, Ezra 3:2-3, 10. But sacrifice and worship had not come to a standstill in Jerusalem during the exile. Though the Temple was no more, the place where it had stood remained a holy place. According to Jeremiah 41:5, after the destruction of Jerusalem people came from Shechem, Shiloh and Samaria with cereal offerings and incense to present at the temple of the Lord. People from the territory of tribes which had never belonged to the kingdom of Judah came to the central sanctuary. It is very likely that worship of some form continued to take place where the Temple had been.

However the people who continued worship in Jerusalem during the exile were not the exiled community, the *gôlāh*, through whom the Chronicler wished to trace the continuance of Israel's faith and the resumption of sacrifice in the holy place. Nor could "the opponents of Judah and Benjamin," "the people of the land," assist in the rebuilding,

Ezra 4:1-5. According to the Chronicler it was the people of the land alone who frustrated the building of the Temple "throughout all the lifetime of Cyrus the king of Persia and even until the reign of Darius the king of Persia" (Ezra 4:5). The Chronicler then inserts two examples of obstruction and interference, but taken from *later* times, one from the beginning of the reign of Xerxes, v. 6, the other from the time of Artaxerxes I, vv. 7-24. He then concludes, "Then the work on the house of God which is in Jerusalem stopped; and it ceased until the second year of the reign of Darius king of Persia," v. 24. Who were these people of the land? The Chronicler makes it quite clear that he is thinking exclusively of Samaria when he speaks of the "people of the land." They are the ruling classes, the Samaritans who had occupied the land, not the upper classes of Judah.

With the death of Cambyses in 522 there was a rumble of revolt in the Persian Empire. Darius, Cambyses' successor who had been with him in Syria, spent about a year back in the eastern provinces quelling disturbances. It was only towards the end of 521 that he established himself securely. These disturbances seem to have given occasion to the prophets Haggai and Zechariah to urge the building of the Temple and to pronounce some of their messianic hopes. Haggai delivered his five (or six) oracles in August-December 520, Hag 1:1. Zechariah spoke between 520 and 518, Zech 1:1, 7; 7:1, and shortly before the dedication of the Temple in 515. Whereas the Chronicler attributed the delay in building the Temple to the opposition of the people of the land, Haggai gives other reasons. The people were too preoccupied with their own difficulties and disappointments, Hag 1:-8-9. Why had there been so little progress since the return? "Because of my house that lies in ruins, while you busy yourselves each with his own house," Hag 1:9. There had been bad harvests, v. 6, and a drought, vv. 10-11, so the people had been even more intent on their own miseries. But the real reason for the poor economic and agricultural state is the neglect of Yahweh and his house. Haggai anticipates a divine intervention in the immediate future together with the installation of the anointed one. The world-shaking events which are a prelude to the eschatological event are at hand, nation destroying nation, Hag 2:6-7; 21-22. There must be a temple to receive Yahweh at his coming. With the restoration of Yahweh's house and with his intervention there will come material prosperity; the wealth of the nations will stream into Zion, Hag 2:6-7. Yet the Temple is but a beginning; it is not everything. What is important is that Yahweh will be with his people, Hag 2:4b-5. With the completion of the Temple and the divine intervention there was to come the installation of the anointed one. He was to be Zerubbabel whom Haggai addresses as the signet ring whom the Lord had chosen, 2:23, seeing in him the survival of the messianic dynasty, a dynasty that was to persevere through the cosmic disturbances which were to herald the setting up of the messianic kingdom, Hag 2:21-22.

Zechariah reflects a similar background. The Temple is in process of being rebuilt, 4:9-10, and this process is both sign and beginning of messianic salvation. As in Haggai 2:5 Yahweh's spirit is the driving force behind the word in 4:6ff. Yahweh's coming is imminent, 2:14, 8:3. The nations will join themselves to Yahweh, 2:15. With Yahweh's saving act comes material prosperity, 8:10-12, and such prosperity that all nations will want to go up to Jerusalem, 8:23. Commentators are in general agreement that "the Branch" of 6:9-14 (*cf.,* 3:8), a messianic title, Jer 23:5; 33:15 (*cf.,* Ps 132[133]:17), refers to Zerubbabel for whose name that of the high priest Joshua was later substituted. It was Zerubbabel who brought the building of the Temple to completion, 4:9-10.

This building activity which the two prophets had stimulated (*cf.,* Ezra 5:2; 6:14) was the occasion of an intervention of Tattenai, the governor of Samaria, and his associates. But the work continued while an appeal was made to Darius who confirmed the edict of Cyrus authorizing the project. The dedication took place in the sixth year of the reign of Darius, 515. Ezra 2:36-58 lists the descendants of the clerical families who could legitimately prove their origin and had returned to Jerusalem. Well before the dedication of the Temple in 515 there were over five thousand of this group who had returned as well as about 35,000 other repatriates. It is likely that even before the official resumption of the cult they had begun to insist on legal practices and observances. But when it is a question of fasting, Zechariah gives the traditional reply of the pre-exilic prophets — he who fasts must not seek his own self-interest, 7:2-7; he must practice justice and true charity, 7:8ff. The *fact* of the return was the driving motive for the utterance of the oracles. Haggai on the other hand speaks immediately out of the eschatological tradition.

The general situation of Jerusalem-Judah in the period 521-515 may be summed up: 1) materially and politically: the city's walls are still down, the Temple is in ruins but is being rebuilt; the economic and agricultural situation is poor. 2) liturgically: there was sacrifice on the former Temple site; even in the short time since the return an exaggerated insistence on ritual and legal prescriptions had obsessed some and had obscured justice and charity. 3) theologically: the divine eschatological intervention is at hand and Yahweh's anointed will be set up on Zion. This is to bring with it material prosperity; the wealth of the nations will come into Zion, and the nations themselves will worship there. Yahweh's imminent coming demands a Temple to receive him. The day on which blessing begins for the people is the day on which the foundation stone of the Temple is laid, Hag 2:15-19.

There is comparatively little information about Judah from the dedication of the Temple in 515 down to the arrival of Nehemiah in the 20th year of Artaxerxes I in 445. The prophecy of Malachi, unless one dates it in the last quarter of the 5th century, may reflect in however limited a way the situation in this period. After the dedication one can only assume that the friction between the repatriates and the people of the land continued, *cf.,* Ezra 3:3; 4:5; Hag 2:4; Zech 8:10. The resentment of the Samaritans at the exclusion from any share in the building of the Temple could only become deeper, Ezra 4:3, *cf.,* Neh 2:20. When Nehemiah arrived in 445 with a commission from Artaxerxes to build the walls, he immediately met with opposition from Sanballat, the governor of Samaria, and his followers, Neh 2:19-20; 4:1-3, 7-8; 6:1-19. There were also disputes among "the brethren" themselves, Neh 5. It was a question of lending and borrowing, or mortgaging, of marrying and giving in marriage in order to eat and live. Some of the community had become wealthy by using every available opportunity to further their own interests and by victimizing their fellow Jews. Apparently they conspired and intermarried with the people of the land. Under Nehemiah's first administration there was a general cancellation of debts and taxes and a return of property that had been pledged. Later Ezra regulated the matter of mixed marriages. The situation about 445 then was this: with Nehemiah's arrival in this year Jerusalem-Judah became a separate province; the Temple is well established, the liturgy is being carried out, the community is well in the direction of becoming a "temple community"; there is a distinct consciousness of the importance of law and the fulfilment of legal prescriptions; the walls are restored under Nehemiah's direction; the community is turning in upon itself spiritually and geographically. One must find such a situation and mentality in Isa 56-66 in order to set them in a period close to Nehemiah's.

2. Literary-Religious Background

It was Bernhard Duhm (1892) who separated chaps. 56-66 from chaps. 40-55 and thus "created Trito-Isaiah." The prophet, according to Duhm, was a contemporary of Ezra and wrote about the middle of the 5th century; he had the spirit of Ezekiel of whom he made so much use and he borrowed verbally from Isaiah 1-55, Jeremiah and Job. He had three tasks, all foreign to Second Isaiah: 1) to point out to the people their sins, 2) to bring the good news to the poor, 3) to proclaim the day of salvation and vengeance. He was one single author who was responsible for the whole of chaps. 56-66 apart from a few later additions.

The half century of scholarship following Duhm saw no unanimity as to authorship, date and construction of chaps. 56-66; passages were distributed across five centuries, from the time of Manasseh in the 7th century to the time of the Maccabees in the 2nd. In recent decades however there has emerged a broad consensus which regards chaps. 56-66 by and large as the work of a single prophet in the generation immediately after the exile, that is in the period 538-500, give or take a few years. This prophet knew well the writings of the great Isaiah of the 8th century and the work of the prophet of the exile; he resumed, adapted and applied words, phrases and verses from chaps. 40-55 to the post-exilic situation in Jerusalem and Judah.

The nucleus of the message of chaps. 56-66 is found in chaps. 60-62 which are a literary unit and whose theme is salvation and salvation alone, that is Yahweh's intervention on behalf of his people and its consequences. They are framed by two community laments, 59:1-20 and 63:7-64:12, whose place of origin is Israel's liturgical worship. There are some unconnected utterances also dealing exclusively with salvation, 57:14-10; 65:16b-25; 66:1-16. Already in the post-exilic community there was a division between the pious and those who opposed them, 56:9-57:13; 57:21; 59:2-8; 65:1-16a; 66:3-4, 5, 17. The attitude to the nations in chaps. 56-66 is friendly; however there is a strand running through which speaks of judgment on the nations, 60:12; 63:1-6; 66:6-7, 15-16, 20, 22, 23; there are also what are best described as apocalyptic additions, 60:19-20; 65:17, 15; 66:20, 23-24. The whole of the eleven chapters are framed by passages which show great openness to the gentiles, 56:1-2; 3-8; 66:18-19, 21.

Evidence for the dating of chaps. 56-66 is internal, that is, it is taken from the text itself. Remembering always that the prophets of the Old Testament took over stereotyped phrases and images, that they also reworked in varying degrees blocks of material at hand to them, we may summarize the evidence for dating taken from the text itself as follows:

1. The temple is in ruins and the new temple is still to be built: 60:7-13; 63:18; 64:10; 66:1.
2. The city, the walls and the surrounding cities are in ruins: 58:2; 60:10, 15; 61:4; 63:18; 64:9-10.
3. Economic and legal conditions are desperate, justice is neglected: 57:1-2; 58:6-7, 9-10; 59:4, 9, 14; 62:8-9; 65:13-14.
4. Foreigners dominate: 62:8-9; 65:13-14, 21-23.
5. No king, no ruler, no organized community: 63:19.
6. Gross neglect on the part of those responsible: 56:10-12.
7. Jerusalem is to be the centre of the future, the nations will flock to Zion: 56:8; 60-62; 65:18-19; 66:7ff, 10f.
8. Canaanite abuses are widespread: 57:1-13; 65:3-7; 66:3-4.
9. Eschatological expectations: the future will be the reverse of the present: 60-62; 62:2b; 65:17ff; 66:7ff, 10f.
10. Yahweh will come to the humble and broken in spirit: 57:15b, 61:1; 66:2.
11. The theme of joy in the eschatological age: 61:10-11; 62:5; 65:18-19; 66:10.
12. Points of contact with Haggai and Zechariah:
    a) temple soon to be built: Hag *passim*, Zech 4:9-10; 1-16
    b) eschatological intervention: Hag 2:6
    c) wealth of nations comes to Zion: Hag 2:6-9; Zech 2:13
    d) nations come to Zion: Zech 2:15; 8:23.
    e) echoes of Zech 7:13 in Is 65:1, 12b; 66:4
    f) Jerusalem the centre of the future: Hag 2:6-9

Nos. 1-6 reflect a situation which conforms well with what we know to have been the state of Jerusalem round about 520. The factors are reasonably distributed throughout the eleven chapters, though more pronounced in the last seven. Canaanite abuses are as old as the Israelite settlement in

Palestine so that nothing very much can be concluded from them as to date, except that they persevered after the exile. Chaps. 60-66 are dominated by Jerusalm-Zion as the centre of the future and the joy and judgment that follow Yahweh's definitive intervention. The themes of nos. 9 and 11 are well distributed. Then there are the points of contact with Haggai and Zechariah whose dates are well established.

There is then a situation reflected in chaps. 56-66 that corresponds to what we know of Jerusalem about 520. The identifying factors are spread evenly throughout. The chapters present a number of historical and historical-theological points of contact with Haggai and Zechariah who made their pronouncements around 520. The chapters may therefore be set at approximately the same period. The substance and arrangement point to one author, due allowance being made for the taking over of blocks of material already at hand (*e.g.*, 63:7-64:12) and some later additions. The passages do not develop a continuous theme in a direct line but are rather separate pieces grouped around the same historical situation and repeating a common theology, spoken at different times into and out of the prophet's milieu according to need.

56:1-8. THE TRUE PEOPLE OF GOD

56 Thus says the LORD:
"Keep justice, and do righteousness,
for soon my salvation will come,
and my deliverance be revealed.
[2]Blessed is the man who does this,
and the son of man who holds it fast,
who keeps the sabbath, not profaning it,
and keeps his hand from doing any evil."

[3]Let not the foreigner who has joined himself to the LORD say,
"The LORD will surely separate me from his people";

and let not the eunuch say,
"Behold, I am a dry tree."
[4]For thus says the LORD:
"To the eunuchs who keep my sabbaths,
who choose the things that please me
and hold fast my covenant,
[5]I will give in my house and within my walls
a monument and a name
better than sons and daughters;
I will give them an everlasting name
which shall not be cut off.

[6]"And the foreigners who join themselves to the LORD,
to minister to him, to love the name of the LORD,
and to be his servants,
every one who keeps the sabbath, and does not profane it,
and holds fast my covenant —
[7]these I will bring to my holy mountain,
and make them joyful in my house of prayer;
their burnt offerings and their sacrifices
will be accepted on my altar;
for my house shall be called a house of prayer
for all peoples.
[8]Thus says the LORD GOD,
who gathers the outcasts of Israel,
I will gather yet others to him
besides those already gathered."

We have in these eight verses a prophetic Torah, that is, a religious instruction, a making known the will of Yahweh. The prophet does not take it upon himself to instruct but takes his stand on Yahweh, pointing three times to him as the source of the instruction, vv. 1a, 4a, 8a. He is Yahweh's channel of communication. The gates of the Temple in which God's people worship are being opened to those considered to be beyond the pale, Deut 23:1-8.

vv. 1-2. The chapter begins abruptly with the messenger formula, "thus says Yahweh" (v. 1ai), followed by the message. The people are to observe *mishpat* and so *sedaqah*, that is they are to do as they should as members of God's covenant people *because* God's saving action, *yeshu'ah* and *sedaqah*, is near, not in order to bring it about. The half-verse recalls Second Isaiah 46:13 where Yahweh calls on his people to attend because his saving action is at hand. The proper order to be observed includes the sabbath now resumed in the blessing of v. 2. Though observance of the sabbath became a distinctive sign of post-exilic Judaism enforced by Nehemiah, 13:15ff, it was an ancient tradition. It is mentioned in all the codes of law in the Pentateuch, Exod 23:12 (Elohistic code); Exod 34:21 (Yahwistic code); Exod 31:12-17 (Priestly code); Deut 5:12-14 and Exod 20:8-10 (the two redactions of the decalogue), was a matter of concern to the 8th century prophets, Amos 8:5; Hos 2:11; Isa 1:13, and its violation an accusation that Ezekiel launched at the people of Israel, Ezek 20:13; 22:25; 25:28.

vv. 3-7. The verses seem to presume a community fortified by laws. Certain foreigners, Ammonites and Moabites, could not enter the assembly of the Lord, Deut 23:3-5; Neh 13:1-3. The problem however had its beginnings well before the return from Babylon to Jerusalem. We read in Jeremiah that shortly after the destruction of the city, "....all the Jews who were in Moab and among the Ammonites and in Edom and in other lands....returned from all the places to which they had been driven and came to the land of Judah, to Gedeliah at Mizpah," Jer 40:11-12. Foreigners may well have come to Judah with these Jews who themselves could well have been contaminated by pagan practices. As for the eunuchs, the position of cup-bearer at the Persian court was held by a eunuch, and one may infer that Nehemiah was such. This too may have been the fate of some of the exiles who according to Deut 23:1 could not join the worshipping assembly. Such is the raw material for the admission of foreigners and eunuchs to the Temple. A divine oracle is required to set aside or adapt the law and this would be given by a priest or prophet. Verses 3-7 are a later application of the universality of Second Isaiah and reach a climax in v. 7, "for my house shall be called a house of prayer by (for) all peoples," *cf.*, the universality of 1 Kgs 8:41.

The words rendered "a monument and a name" in v. 5 are literally "a hand and a name." The word *yad*, hand, is used in a number of well known texts for a monument, in 1 Sam 15:12 for Saul's monument; the pillar which Absolom set up to keep his name in remembrance because he had no son "is called Absolom's monument (*yad*) to this day," 2 Sam 18:18. In the excavations at Hazor about 9m. north of the lake of Galilee Yigael Yadin found some stone columns with hands carved on them in a funerary shrine. The "hand," *i.e.*, what is carved on the stele, hence the name and personality of the bearer, shall never be "cut off" or "effaced," as certain Egyptian Pharaohs "cut out" or "effaced" the inscribed names of their predecessors. The following version of 56:5 is proposed:

> And in my house, yes within my walls,
> I will set up an inscribed stele to them,
> better than sons and daughters.
> I shall put an everlasting memorial upon it,
> which shall never be effaced.

A number of authors however prefer a less material explanation and think that the words are a picturesque way of saying that the people in question will be admitted to the temple.

v. 8. "The outcasts of Israel" are the "scattered of Israel." In Ps 147(146-147):2 they are the whole people and in Isa 11:12 they are parallel to the dispersed of Judah. To the true Israel now gathered in Jerusalem Yahweh will add others.

The whole passage, comprising some three or four oracles, belongs probably to the early post-exilic period, 521-515, as the second Temple was being built.

56:9 57:13
WICKED LEADERS AND FALSE WORSHIP

[9]All you beasts of the field, come to devour —
all you beasts in the forest.
[10]His watchmen are blind,
they are all without knowledge;
they are all dumb dogs,
they cannot bark;
dreaming, lying down,
loving to slumber.
[11]The dogs have a mighty appetite;
they never have enough.
The shepherds also have no understanding;
they have all turned to their own way,
each to his own gain, one and all.
[12]"Come," they say, "let us get wine,
let us fill ourselves with strong drink;
and tomorrow will be like this day,
great beyond measure."

57The righteous man perishes,
and no one lays it to heart;
devout men are taken away,
while no one understands.
for the righteous man is taken away from calamity,
[2]he enters into peace;
they rest in their beds
who walk in their uprightness.
[3]But you, draw near hither,
sons of the sorceress,
offspring of the adulterer and the harlot.
[4]Of whom are you making sport?
Against whom do you open your mouth wide
and put out your tongue?
Are you not children of transgression,
the offspring of deceit,
[5]you who burn with lust among the oaks,
under every green tree;

who slay your children in the valleys,
under the clefts of the rocks?
[6]Among the smooth stones of the valley is your portion;
they, they, are your lot;
to them you have poured out a drink offering,
you have brought a cereal offering.
Shall I be appeased for these things?
[7]Upon a high and lofty mountain
you have set your bed,
and thither you went up to offer sacrifice.
[8]Behind the door and the doorpost
you have set up your symbol;
for, deserting me, you have uncovered your bed,
you have gone up to it,
you have made it wide;
and you have made a bargain for yourself with them,
you have loved their bed,
you have looked on nakedness.
[9]You journeyed to Molech with oil
and multiplied your perfumes;
you sent your envoys far off.
and sent down even to Sheol.
[10]You were wearied with the length of your way,
but you did not say, "It is hopeless";
you found new life for your strength,
and so you were not faint.
[11]Whom did you dread and fear,
so that you lied,
and did not remember me,
did not give me a thought?
Have I not held my peace, even for a long time,
and so you do not fear me?
[12]I will tell of your righteousness and your doings,
but they will not help you.
[13]When you cry out, let your collection of idols deliver
you!
The wind will carry them off,
a breath will take them away.

> But he who takes refuge in me shall possess the land,
> and shall inherit my holy mountain.

The religious leaders of the people, 56:9-12, and the faithless of Israel, 57:3-13, are the two groups addressed; the proclamations of judgment against them are linked by two verses (57:1-2) which lament the lot of the just. The prophet is resuming traditional prophetic material and applying it to the situation he faces.

vv. 9-12. The speaker, or perhaps Yahweh, calls on the beasts of the field to devour the people, unprotected by their faithless leaders, "the shepherds and watchmen." A century before Jeremiah had written:

> Go, assemble all the wild beasts; bring them to devour.
> Many shepherds have destroyed my vineyard,
> they have trampled down my portion,
> they have made my pleasant portion a desolate wilderness.
> Jer 12:9b-10

The author was aware of the situation in Jeremiah's time. It is the same in the early post-exilic period and the shepherds are again to blame. Yahweh's heritage is still fit only to be destroyed and preyed upon by wild beasts, and this because of the conduct of the religious leaders who neglect their office (v. 10) and are intent on their own self-interest and pleasure (v. 11). The prophet puts on their lips some lines from a drinking song (v. 12) which recalls the well known song quoted in Isaiah 22:13, "let us eat and drink, for tomorrow we die," taken up by Paul in 1 Cor 15:32, and the Roman poet Horace's "Enjoy the Passing Hour!" — ". . . . why not rather quaff the wine. . . . Bacchus dispels gnawing cares. . ." Odes 2,11.

57:1-2. This slowly moving lament that the pious are perishing from the land while no one cares has its parallels in Ps 12(11):1 and Mic 7:2. Verses 1b-2 are difficult: "they rest in their beds" is in the plural, "walk in uprightness" in the singular. The word for bed, *mishkab*, has the well attested meaning of grave or eternal resting place both in the Bible and in west semitic inscriptions. The ultimate lot of the just will be peaceful.

vv. 3-13. The passage may be divided conveniently in this way:

3	call to judgment and accusation of infidelity
4-6	elaboration of accusation in the form of a trial speech
7-10	further elaboration of accusation and proof
11	guilt is established
12-13b	their own perversity has condemned them
13c	a word of comfort for all

Children of a sorceress (*cf.,* Isa 2:6; Mic 5:11; Jer 27:9), of adulterers and harlots, v. 3, are the descendants of those unfaithful to the (marriage) alliance between Yahweh and his people, children who are no better than those castigated by the 8th century prophets and Jeremiah. The gestures referred to in v. 4 are rude gestures of contempt which mock Yahweh's faithful. The reference in v. 5a is to Canaanite rites with their sexual overtones, and in v. 5b to the abominable child sacrifice. This first appears in Israel in the first half of the 9th century under King Ahab. Israel witnessed Mesha, king of Moab, sacrifice his son on the city wall when the battle was going against him, 2 Kgs 3:27, and King Ahaz of Judah "even burned his son as an offering, according to the abominable practices of the nations. . . . he sacrificed and burned incense on the high places, and on the hills, and under every green tree," 2 Kgs 16:3-4. This practice was abolished by Josiah in his reform in the latter part of the 7th century, 2 Kgs 23:10. However it seems to have come to light again with renewed vigour after the failure of the reform, Jer 7:31.

There is a change of person in v. 6. Hitherto the address had been in the second person masculine plural, but now, in vv. 6-13, it is in the second person feminine singular; Israel is spoken to as the spouse married to Yahweh by covenant.

The "smooth stones" of v. 6b are a problem. Reading the same Hebrew letters, but a different root, the following has been proposed: "with the dead of the wadi is your portion; they, they are your lot."

Verses 7-9 describe the idolatrous Canaanite cults practised by Israel on the mountains. The "symbol" of v. 8a probably refers to a representation of a phallus; v. 8b may be rendered:

> Yes, you have divorced me, you have gone up
> and widened your bed,
> You have made yourself a (covenant of) bed-loving,
> you have gazed on lust.

By repointing the Hebrew consonants in v. 9a the NEB reads, "You drenched your tresses in oil, blended with many perfumes." Molech of the RSV is *melek*, king, in the traditional Hebrew text; this is a divine title applied to many deities in the ancient semitic world. The context here is that of the underworld, Sheol, and in Job 18:14 *melek* is an epithet of *Môt*, death. Is it a matter of necromancy? And despite the futility of it all the idolaters continue their practices, v. 10. It is not easy to follow the line of thought in v. 11. The following analysis is proposed:

11ai	whom do you fear or reverence when you perform all this, *i.e.*, this false worship of vv. 3-10. Me?
11aii	No, it is not me you fear. You are lying.
11b	You don't fear or think of me at all!
11ci	and why do you not fear me? because I have not brought the sort of glorious restoration you want; because I am silent and bide my time.
11cii	and so you don't fear me; you turn to other gods.

Yahweh will declare, make public these false acts of cult. The idols they have cultivated will be of no avail. Verses 12-13a are rendered:

> I will proclaim your deeds, your self-justifying acts;
> But they will not help you,
> will not save you when you cry out, these idols of yours.

What Yahweh requires is loyalty to the covenant and that worship which is a consequence of covenant loyalty. Verse 13c is a word for all, and the inheritance of the holy mountain follows on fidelity to the covenant.

It is not possible to date 56:9 - 57:13 by means of content. The aberrations denounced have been there throughout the whole history of Israel, though they would fit quite well the reign of Manasseh, 687-642, 2 Kgs 21. It is much more likely that we have here pieces of prophetic tradition re-worked and re-applied in a post-exilic situation.

57:14-21.
PEACE, PEACE, TO THE FAR AND TO THE NEAR

> [14]And it shall be said,
> "Build up, build up, prepare the way,
> remove every obstruction from my people's way."
> [15]For thus says the high and lofty One
> who inhabits eternity, whose name is Holy:
> "I dwell in the high and holy place,
> and also with him who is of a contrite and humble spirit,
> to revive the spirit of the humble,
> and to revive the heart of the contrite.
> [16]For I will not contend for ever,
> nor will I always be angry;
> for from me proceeds the spirit,
> and I have made the breath of life.
> [17]Because of the iniquity of his covetousness I was angry,
> I smote him, I hid my face and was angry;
> but he went on backsliding in the way of his own heart.

[18]I have seen his ways, but I will heal him;
I will lead him and requite him with comfort,
creating for his mourners the fruit of the lips.
[19]Peace, peace, to the far and to the near, says the LORD;
and I will heal him.
[20]But the wicked are like the tossing sea;
for it cannot rest,
and its waters toss up mire and dirt.
[21]There is no peace, says my God, for the wicked."

This oracle of salvation relies on and differs from Second Isaiah. The obstruction that stands in "my people's way" (v. 14) is their sin. Yahweh will remove his anger from them, he will heal them and give them prosperity and well-being (*shālôm*).

vv. 14-15. The speaker is Yahweh and the resemblance to 40:3 is obvious. But the way that is to be heaped up is the spiritual way to salvation. The string of present participles, familiar from chaps. 40-55, which are characteristic of descriptive praise, are retained and adapted. Yahweh is "the high and sublime," as in Isa 6:1, who abides for ever; he is both transcendent and close to those who are crushed and bowed down, v. 15. The sense of a God who is remote, Exod 3:3-6; 33:17-23, and who is near, Deut 4:7, went deep into the religion of Israel.

vv. 16-17. The oracle of salvation proper begins here, and is best introduced, "See, I will not always contend. . . ." Why? "because their spirit is faint before me, and the breath of life which is theirs, I, yes I, made it, v. 16b, (not as in RSV). Again, as in Second Isaiah, it is the creator who brings salvation, "he who breathed into human nostrils the breath of life," Gen 2:7. Just as her iniquity, *'awon*, was pardoned, 40:2, so too the iniquity that roused Yahweh's anger and caused him to hide his face is healed.

vv. 18-21. Without any emendation of the Hebrew consonants and by regrouping the words, vv. 18-19 read:

I have seen his ways, but I will heal him and give him rest,
I will give full consolation to him and his mourners,

(*bārā'*) as the utterance (flow) of his lips,
'Peace, peace to the far and near.'
Yes, I will heal him, says Yahweh.

Overflowing prosperity will accompany God's saving action; he alone creates for the far and near, *i.e.*, for all, as in Isa 33:13, not for two groups, exiles and non-exiles. But the wicked, those in revolt, are like the troubled sea and cannot share God's peace and prosperity. Verse 21 is a slight adaptation of 48:22.

58:1-14. TRUE SERVICE AND TRUE FASTING

58 "Cry aloud, spare not,
lift up your voice like a trumpet;
declare to my people their transgression,
to the house of Jacob their sins.
[2]Yet they seek me daily,
and delight to know my ways,
as if they were a nation that did righteousness
and did not forsake the ordinance of their God;
they ask of me righteous judgments,
they delight to draw near to God.
[3]'Why have we fasted, and thou seest it not?
Why have we humbled ourselves, and thou takest no knowledge of it?"
Behold, in the day of your fast you seek your own pleasure,
and oppress all your workers.
[4]Behold, you fast only to quarrel and to fight
and to hit with wicked fist.
Fasting like yours this day will not make your voice to be heard on high.
[5]Is such the fast that I choose,
a day for a man to humble himself?
Is it to bow down his head like a rush,
and to spread sackcloth and ashes under him?

Will you call this a fast,
and a day acceptable to the LORD?

[6]"Is not this the fast that I choose:
to loose the bonds of wickedness,
to undo the thongs of the yoke,
to let the oppressed go free,
and to break every yoke?
[7]Is it not to share your bread with the hungry,
and bring the homeless poor into your house;
when you see the naked, to cover him,
and not to hide yourself from your own flesh?
[8]Then shall your light break forth like the dawn,
and your healing shall spring up speedily;
your righteousness shall go before you,
the glory of the LORD shall be your rear guard.
[9]Then you shall call, and the LORD will answer;
you shall cry, and he will say, Here I am.
"If you take away from the midst of you the yoke,
the pointing of the finger, and speaking wickedness,
[10]if you pour yourself out for the hungry
and satisfy the desire of the afflicted,
then shall your light rise in the darkness
and your gloom be as the noonday.
[11]And the LORD will guide you continually,
and satisfy your desire with good things,
and make your bones strong;
and you shall be like a watered garden,
like a spring of water,
whose waters fail not.
[12]And your ancient ruins shall be rebuilt;
you shall raise up the foundations of many generations;
you shall be called the repairer of the breach,
the restorer of streets to dwell in.

[13]"If you turn back your foot from the sabbath,
from doing your pleasure on my holy day,
and call the sabbath a delight
and the holy day of the LORD honorable;

if you honor it, not going your own ways,
or seeking your own pleasure, or talking idly;
[14]then you shall take delight in the LORD,
and I will make you ride upon the heights of the earth;
I will feed you with the heritage of Jacob your father,
for the mouth of the LORD has spoken."

Several strands of prophetic tradition coalesce in this liturgy over which the prophet presides. The people were accustomed to come together in times of national crisis to hold fasts, Josh 7:6; Judg 20:26; 1 Sam 7:6; 1 Kgs 21:12; Jer 36:9; Joel 1:1-2:27; Ps 35(34):13; 1 Macc 3:47. They now assemble in a city still in ruins, v. 12, and complain that they have observed punctiliously the ritual fast, but God has not intervened, has not brought that prosperity and well being he had promised. The prophet answers the complaint.

vv. 1-3a. The prophet conveys the call of Yahweh in language typical of 8th century prophecy, Hos 8:1; Mic 3:16. The people follow the prescribed ritual "like (not 'as if' in RSV) a nation that has done what is proper (*sedaqah*) and has not forsaken the ordinance (*mishpat*) of its God; they have asked me for ordinances of conduct (*mishpĕtê sedeq*) and they delight to be near to God," v. 2b-c. The people think that they are doing what is required and look for instructions that will put them on the way of *sedeq*, in favour with God. But nothing happens.

vv. 3b-5. Another element is now introduced, familiar from the 8th century prophets: people fulfill the ritual while going their own way, oppressing the less fortunate and quarrelling over business. Their lives do not conform with the spirit of fasting. Neither this nor sheer ritualism is what God requires. Samuel had long ago told Saul that "to obey is better than sacrifice," 1 Sam 15:22 (though sacrifice is not mentioned here) and Amos and Micah had excoriated the oppressors of the poor and needy, Amos 4:1, 4-5; 5:11-13; 8:4-6; Mic 6:10ff, and had condemned ritual when substituted for justice, Amos 5:21-23.

vv. 6-9a. Loyalty to God consists above all in that due order, *mishpat* and *sedaqah*, that preserves harmony in the community and sees that each person, no matter who, is justly treated. Here, as so often with a people turned in upon itself, justice and concern are left aside. But fasting cannot be substituted for compassion. Release from any sort of bondage is a primary concern, v. 6, and Israel ought to remember that she has just returned from two generations of bondage. The requirements of v. 7 are obligations widely accepted in the ancient Near East and in Israel; to observe them is to do *mishpat* and *sedaqah*; people are more important than cultic rites, no matter how sincerely these latter are directed towards God. Verses 7-9a are a conditional construction saying that "if you share. . . . then your light . . . . then you shall call. . . ."; that is, if you do *mishpat* and *sedaqah*, your own *sedaqah* (RSV righteousness) "shall go before you and the glory of the Lord (*kābôd*) shall be your rear guard"; God's saving presence shall be among his people. This verse, 9a, is a resumption and reworking of 52:12b where "the Lord God will go before you, and the God of Israel will be your rear guard."

vv. 9b-12. These verses are again a conditional construction along the same lines as vv. 7-9a. "If you take away. . . . if you pour yourself out. . . . then the Lord will guide you . . . . and your ancient ruins. . . ." The yoke is any form of oppression and the pointing of the finger is to make false accusations in the same way as those "who turn justice upside down," Amos 5:7; *cf.,* Prov 6:12-14; the similies are traditional.

vv. 13-14. There is the same structure here as in the previous passage. For the sabbath, see comments on 56:2. The sabbath is to be the outward expression of inner dedication to God. The verses can be readily related to vv. 1-2. The people allege that they seek God's pleasure, vv. 1-2. That this is not so is made clear in the verses that follow. What is God's pleasure? It is a combination of *mishpat* and *sedaqah*, vv. 6-9a, 9b-10a, *i.e.,* true justice, and true religious observance, v. 13.

The situation faced by the prophet in vv. 3-5 is very like that which Zechariah faced in the fourth year of King Darius, 519-518, Zech 7:4-12. This, together with the references to the state of the city in 58:12, and with no sign of the Temple, would justify the setting of the passage in the six or seven years before the dedication of the second Temple in 515.

59:1-21.
INJUSTICE AND WRONGDOING

59 Behold, the Lord's hand is not shortened,
that it cannot save,
or his ear dull, that it cannot hear;
[2]but your iniquities have made a separation
between you and your God,
and your sins have hid his face from you so that he does not hear.
[3]For your hands are defiled with blood
and your fingers with iniquity;
your lips have spoken lies, your tongue mutters wickedness.
[4]No one enters suit justly,
no one goes to law honestly;
they rely on empty pleas, they speak lies,
they conceive mischief and bring forth iniquity.
[5]They hatch adders' eggs,
they weave the spider's web;
he who eats their eggs dies,
and from one which is crushed a viper is hatched.
[6]Their webs will not serve as clothing;
men will not cover themselves with what they make.
Their works are works of iniquity,
and deeds of violence are in their hands.
[7]Their feet run to evil,
and they make haste to shed innocent blood;
their thoughts are thoughts of iniquity,
desolation and destruction are in their highways.

[8]The way of peace they know not,
and there is no justice in their paths;
they have made their roads crooked,
no one who goes in them knows peace.

[9]Therefore justice is far from us,
and righteousness does not overtake us;
we look for light, and behold, darkness,
and for brightness, but we walk in gloom.
[10]We grope for the wall like the blind,
we grope like those who have no eyes;
we stumble at noon as in the twilight,
among those in full vigor we are like dead men.
[11]We all growl like bears,
we moan and moan like doves;
we look for justice, but there is none;
for salvation, but it is far from us.
[12]For our transgressions are multiplied before thee,
and our sins testify against us;
for our transgressions are with us,
and we know our iniquities:
[13]transgressing, and denying the LORD,
and turning away from following our God,
speaking oppression and revolt,
conceiving and uttering from the heart lying words.
[14]Justice is turned back,
and righteousness stands afar off;
for truth has fallen in the public squares,
and uprightness cannot enter.
[15]Truth is lacking,
and he who departs from evil makes himself a prey.

The LORD saw it, and it displeased him
that there was no justice.
[16]He saw that there was no man,
and wondered that there was no one to intervene;
then his own arm brought him victory,
and his righteousness upheld him.
[17]He put on righteousness as a breastplate,

and a helmet of salvation upon his head;
he put on garments of vengeance for clothing,
and wrapped himself in fury as a mantle.
[18]According to their deeds, so will he repay,
wrath to his adversaries, requital to his enemies;
to the coastlands he will render requital.
[19]So they shall fear the name of the LORD from the west,
and his glory from the rising of the sun;
for he will come like a rushing stream,
which the wind of the LORD drives.
[20]And he will come to Zion as Redeemer,
to those in Jacob who turn from transgression, says the LORD.

[21]"And as for me, this is my covenant with them, says the LORD: my spirit which is upon you, and my words which I have put in your mouth, shall not depart out of your mouth, or out of the mouth of your children, or out of the mouth of your children's children, says the LORD, from this time forth and for evermore."

This poem is a unity (for v. 21 see comment). The community has lamented that Yahweh has not intervened with his saving hand, has not even heard them. The prophet takes up their lament and tells them that it is not any shortcoming on Yahweh's part that is the cause of their present plight, but sin and sin alone, vv. 1-8. The prophet calls implicitly for repentance. The people confess their sins, vv. 9-15a, where all the verbs are in the 1st person plural. Finally the prophet takes the word again: God turns to his people and intervenes as redeemer, vv. 15b-20. A constant change of subject is normal is such exchanges: vv. 1-3, 2nd person plural; vv. 4-8, 3rd person plural (v. 4a in singular, "no one"); v. 9-15a, "we"; vv. 15b-20, Yahweh is subject except for v. 19a, "they shall fear," because of Yahweh's appearance in judgment. This shift in subject does not destroy the unity of the whole, nor do the different literary forms which are mingled together as in the Psalter. Community lament and prophetic voice are interwoven. James Muilenburg has noted how rich and varied is the vocabulary for sin: iniquities, sins, lies, blood, wickedness, chaos (*tohû*, v. 4b, "empty words" RSV), trouble, deeds of violence, transgressions, denying the Lord, turning away from following God. These last two arc of thc cssencc of sin.

There is no reason to think that the audience addressed is other than that in chap. 58. Hence, with due caution, the passage may be set in the early post-exilic period and before the dedication of the Temple in 515.

vv. 1-8. The prophet answers the complaint of the community lament in words that recall 50:1c-2b. Yahweh's power is not restricted nor is he incapable of hearing. The iniquities and sins of the people are the barrier to his presence (face, *pānim*, perhaps an equivalent for God himself); the charge is laid against them in vv. 2-3, and in vv. 4ff there is the transition from the charge to a description of the general state of wickedness. "No one enters suit justly" (v. 4); as the Hebrew has it, "no one calling *bĕsedeq*," the same phrase as in 42:6; 45:13, but here used in a different context and sense. The language of v. 4b is that of the psalms, Pss 12(11):2-3; 42(40):7; 144(143):8, while the last sentence of the verse, "they conceive mischief and bring forth iniquity," is found in Job 15:35. The remaining verses elaborate the state of wickedness in general terms. As a result of this "they do not know the way that brings true welfare (*shālôm*), and there is no acting as is proper (*mishpat*) in their paths," v. 8.

vv. 9-15a. The confession is now introduced. The word *mishpat*, used in v. 8 in the sense of proper conduct, is here, v. 9, joined with *sedaqah*; God's saving action is far from the community, so they stumble around aimlessly and mutter because *mishpat* and *yeshu'ah* (salvation) are far from them, v.11. The confession proper is made in v. 12 which is almost certainly an old liturgical formula, and v. 13a, "turning away from following our God," describes in essense what sin is all about. The words *mishpat* and *sedaqah* are taken up again in v. 14, but in a different context and refer more likely to improper conduct in the public domain. John L. McKenzie sums up the situation well:

> The rebellion and the denial are here seen as being the refusal to accept the moral will of Yahweh. Thus justice, righteousness, fidelity, and sincerity, the ingredients of Yahweh's moral will and the qualities which establish a morally integral community, are excluded.

vv. 15b-20. Just as the confession, vv. 9-15a, was clamped to the elaboration of sins by *mishpat* (RSV justice) in vv. 8a and 9a, so is the divine intervention, vv. 15b-20, clamped to the confession by the same word in vv. 14a and 15b. Yahweh was displeased that the life of the community was not properly ordered, that there was no *mishpat* (RSV justice). There was no one to intervene. The language of v. 16a is almost identical with that of 63:5 where Yahweh identifies himself as one returning from single-handed victory over Israel's enemies. This language and the imagery that goes with it is used here in vv. 16-19 to describe Yahweh coming with his saving action within his own people. Yahweh's power (his arm) and his saving action, *sedaqah*, intervene. Yahweh's intervention is always both judgment and salvation — judgment to those who remain firm in their opposition, salvation for those "who turn from transgression." Yahweh is frequently portrayed as a warior in the Old Testament, and the warrior imagery and armament is taken up in Wis 5:17 and Eph 6:14-17.

v. 21. Many consider the final verse a later addition. Bernhard Duhm thinks that it is an imitation of the priestly style and presents the ideal of legalism; the covenant, he says, is the law, and the spirit is not the spirit that is at work in the servant, nor the prophetic spirit, nor the spirit that leads Israel; it is probably the spirit of obedience. Another writer, W. Kessler, says that the verse would come from a time when the "word" was understood no longer in a prophetic but a nomistic sense. Both of these observations are wide of the mark. The verse, probably a later reflection, must be seen both in the immediate context of chaps. 59 & 60-62 and in the general context of the Isaianic oracles. This is very well expressed by D. R. Jones who understands the verse as a declaration of the complete reliability of the word of God:

> This note is frequently heard in the collection of Isaianic oracles (*cf.*, 31:2; 34:16; 37:36; 40:8; 44:26; 45:19; 48:16; 49:2; 55:10f) and sometimes suggests reflection on the collected oracles, as they are read and considered long after their original utterance. On the other hand, the reference to the inspiration of the spirit in this verse is a characteristic mark of III Isaiah (*cf.*, 61:1ff). This is the final answer to the anxious question of v. 1. The way of the faithful is reliance upon the promises of God; but it also reads like an introduction to chap. 60. When the prophet says THIS IS MY COVENANT WITH THEM, we have to read on into chap. 60 to find out all that is involved.

We might point too to 61:8 where this covenant will be everlasting and to 61:1 where the Spirit of the Lord comes upon the prophet so that he may proclaim the word. The reflection in 59:21 is best understood as a bridge passage.

60:1-22.
ARISE, SHINE O ZION!

60 Arise, shine; for your light has come,
and the glory of the LORD has risen upon you.
[2]For behold, darkness shall cover the earth,
and thick darkness the peoples;
but the LORD will arise upon you,
and his glory will be seen upon you.
[3]And nations shall come to your light,
and kings to the brightness of your rising.

[4]Lift up your eyes round about, and see;
they all gather together, they come to you
your sons shall come from far,
and your daughters shall be carried in the arms.
[5]Then you shall see and be radiant,
your heart shall thrill and rejoice;
because the abundance of the sea shall be turned to you,
the wealth of the nations shall come to you.

[6]A multitude of the camels shall cover you,
the young camels of Midian and Ephah;
all those from Sheba shall come.
They shall bring gold and frankincense,
and shall proclaim the praise of the LORD.
[7]All the flocks of Kedar shall be gathered to you,
the rams of Nebaioth shall minister to you;
they shall come up with acceptance on my altar,
and I will glorify my glorious house.

[8]Who are these that fly like a cloud, and like
doves to their windows?
[9]For the coastlands shall wait for me, the ships of
Tarshish first,
to bring your sons from far,
their silver and gold with them,
for the name of the LORD your God,
and for the Holy One of Israel,
because he has glorified you.

[10]Foreigners shall build up your walls,
and their kings shall minister to you;
for in my wrath I smote you,
but in my favour I have had mercy on you.
[11]Your gates shall be open continually,
day and night they shall not be shut;
that men may bring to you the wealth of the nations,
with their kings led in procession.
[12]For the nation and kingdom
that will not serve you shall perish;
those nations shall be utterly laid waste.
[13]The glory of Lebanon shall come to you,
the cypress, the plane, and the pine,
to beautify the place of my sanctuary;
and I will make the place of my feet glorious.
[14]The sons of those who oppressed you
shall come bending low to you;
and all who despised you
shall bow down at your feet;

they shall call you the City of the LORD,
the Zion of the Holy One of Israel.

[15]Whereas you have been forsaken and hated.
with no one passing through,
I will make you majestic for ever,
a joy from age to age.
[16]You shall suck the milk of nations,
you shall suck the breast of kings;
and you shall know that I, the LORD, am your Savior
and your Redeemer, the Mighty One of Jacob.

[17]Instead of bronze I will bring gold,
and instead of iron I will bring silver;
instead of wood, bronze,
instead of stones, iron.
I will make your overseers peace
and your taskmasters righteousness.
[18]Violence shall no more be heard in your land,
devastation or destruction within your borders;
you shall call your walls Salvation,
and your gates Praise.

[19]The sun shall be no more
your light by day,
nor for brightness shall the moon
give light to you by night;
But the LORD will be your everlasting light,
and your God will be your glory.
[20]Your sun shall no more go down,
nor your moon withdraw itself;
for the LORD will be your everlasting light,
and your days of mourning shall be ended.
[21]Your people shall all be righteous;
they shall possess the land for ever,
the shoot of my planting, the work of my hands,
that I might be glorified.
[22]The least one shall be come a clan,
and the smallest one a mighty nation;
I am the Lord;
in its time I will hasten it.

The theme of chaps. 60-62 is that unique salvation wrought by no one other than Yahweh. These chapters are the centre of the third part of the Book of Isaiah. The present order of chaps. 56-66 does not leave us unprepared for the theme of light which has been introduced already in 58:8a, "then shall your light arise in the darkness, and your gloom be as the noon-day." Chap. 60 is spoken as a word of encouragement to the people in Jerusalem. The trickle of exiles from Babylon has been thin. But Yahweh *has* intervened; it is he who is the speaker throughout, vv. 7b, 9, 10b, 13b, 15b, 16b, 17b, 21b, 22b. This constant recurrence of the 1st person singular, together with the pronoun *ănî*, "I," v. 22b, emphasizes that it is Yahweh alone who effects the saving act and brings glory to Zion; and the nations by bringing their gifts proclaim the glory of Yahweh. Yahweh in action and Zion whom he glorifies are the centre of the picture. One should note too the cultic overtones of the procession: incense is brought, v. 6; countless sheep for the altar, v. 7; timber for the Temple, v. 13. Yahweh is directing the attention of all to the Holy City.

Chap. 60 resume verses from Second Isaiah on a number of occasions: v. 4a resumes 49:18 verbatim; v. 4b modifies 49:22; v. 14a takes up 49:23b almost literally; v. 16a is a modification of 49:23a; v. 16b takes up 46:26, "I, the Lord, am your Saviour and Redeemer, the Mighty One of Jacob"; v. 9c is, except for one word, 55:5b, "for the name (sake) of the Lord your God, and for the Holy One of Israel, because he has beautified you." The Holy One of Israel recurs constantly throughout the sixty six chapters of the Book of Isaiah as it lies before us.

Commentators assess the poetic value of chap. 60 very differently — from James Muilenburg's "superb example of Hebrew literary style" to Bernhard Duhm who, ever ready to disparage the poetic ability of the author of chaps. 56-66, censures the gradual sinking of the level after the outburst of the first four verses. Apart from the obvious prose addition of v. 12 the poetry is of a high standard. Throughout the twenty two verses the proclamation of salvation is interwoven with the description of the future state of the city which enjoys Yahweh's saving intervention rather than with the intervention itself. Zion is bathed in light, vv. 1-3, people move into the procession to Zion, vv. 4-9; there is the rebuilding of the city in vv. 10-16 and a description of her prosperity and peace with a return of the theme of light in vv. 17-22. The themes permeate each other and overlap into the four divisions.

vv. 1-3. The summons to Zion recalls the many imperatives in the Zion poems (51:1-52:12). The theme is Zion in light and the cause of her light is Yahweh and his presence there; the phrase, the glory of Yahweh (*kĕbôd YHWH*) of v. 1, is split into the two parts of the stichos of v. 2b where glory and Yahweh appear in parallelism. Because Yahweh is there in light, all nations and kings shall come to Zion. The two perfects of v. 1, "has come....has risen," better "is come....is risen," are prophetic perfects giving assurance of an action that is still to come.

vv. 4-9. The scattered of Israel are the first in the procession to Zion, v. 4; they comprise not merely the exiles but all who are dispersed, and the effect of their return on Zion is described in the following verse, v. 5a. Then come the nations, vv. 5b-7, whose camel caravans shall fill the land. Without any alteration of the Hebrew consonantal text v. 6aii may be read: "cargoes shall come from Sheba," *i.e.* the ships of the desert, the camels, shall bring their rich cargoes to Zion, *cf.*, the visit of the Queen of Sheba to Solomon (1 Kgs 10:2). The abundance of the sea points north to Tyre and the cities of Phoenicia, the camels of Midian (Gen 37:28, 36) and Ephah (Gen 25:4) point south to the Arabian desert east of the gulf of Aqabah, and Sheba to south Arabia. Kedar and Nebaioth (Gen 25:13) are in north Arabia. Yahweh glorifies himself by the glory with which he crowns Zion. Finally from the west, flying like doves to the dovecotes, come the ships from Tarshish in the south of Spain, *cf.*, Isa 2:16; Ps 48:8; 1 Kgs 10:22; 22:29. As the context seems to require a shipping reference in v. 9, many commentators, with a slight emendation of the text, read "the ships assemble for me" in v. 9a. They will all assist the return of the scattered people of Israel to the glory of Yahweh. This passage with its gold and frankincense and mention of the cities of Arabia is alluded to in Matthew chap. 2 where the wise men come from the east with their gifts and has been used in the Christian Church from the early centuries in the liturgy of the Epiphany.

vv. 10-16. Verse 12 in an addition in prose. The whole city, walls and gates and the Temple, is to be rebuilt and Zion's former oppressors shall supply the material and do the building. As in Second Isaiah this shall be to one purpose, "that you all shall know (experience) that I, the Lord, am your Saviour and your Redeemer, the Mighty One of Jacob," v. 16b. The previous half-verse, v. 16a, with its incongruous "you shall suck the breast of kings," finds a background in the Keret poem from Ugarit in the 14th century, where we read:

> She shall bear Yassib the Lad,
> Who shall draw the milk of A(she)rah,
> Suck the breasts of the maiden Anath,
> The two wet-nurs(es of the gods).
> *(ANET*, p. 146 [ii], 26ff.)

And in the Baal and Anat cycle we find:

> (The gods) eat (and) drink
> And those that suck (the breasts are nourished).
> (C. H. Gordon, *Ugaritic Literature*, p. 30, lines 38-39).

Cyrus Gordon interprets "those who suck" in the light of a carved ivory panel portraying two royal sucklings at the breast of a goddess. The image is not only a symbol of prosperity. It points to royalty being nourished by the gods. So in Isa 60:16 Zion will enjoy royal prosperity which will be given her by Yahweh.

vv. 17-22. The verses describe the state of Zion under Yahweh's saving visitation. The brilliance of Solomon's city and temple will be restored, and the contrast with the future points to the parlous current state of Zion. Once more *shālôm*, peace and well-being, and *sedaqah*, God's saving action and its effect, come together to negate harsh oppression, and the rebuilt wall and gates will assure salvation (prosperity) and renown (praise) — or better, God's saving action will assure the appropriate response, praise of him. From now on Yahweh will be the everlasting light of Zion, vv. 18-19. We may see in vv. 19c and 20b with their repetition that Yahweh "will be their everlasting light," a polemic intent to stress that it is he who holds the foremost place. Here the 1st person singular yields to the name Yahweh. In the Canaanite pantheon Shapsh was the sun goddess and Yarih the moon god. We have already met polemics against Canaanite worship and practices in 57:4-10. After the restoration the people will look to Yahweh, not to Shapsh and Yarih, for blessings. In the Ugaritic poem of Nikkal and Ib we read:

> May the moon shine, and may the moon shine on (for) you.

But Yahweh, not the false deities, is the light and source of blessings for the new Zion.

The people shall be righteous, *saddîq*, that is, they are those through whom Yahweh is to work his saving action, for he is the guardian of his plantation and Zion is the work of his hands which brings him glory. Finally in v. 22 Yahweh reaches back into the patriarchal story where he promised that he would make a mighty nation from Abraham and Sarah, *cf.,* Isa 51:2.

The idea of a procession to or a movement towards Zion is found in Isa 2:2-4 (= Mic 4:1-3) and Hag 2:6-9. The author of Isa 60 is reworking an older tradition but in a different way. In Isa 2:2-4 and the corresponding Micah passage the nations flow to the mountain of the Lord "that he may teach us his ways and that we may walk in his paths." In Isa 60 they come in Yahweh's salvific purpose to rebuild the city and so bring him glory. The language and imagery is much closer to Haggai's, but there is not the same imminent expectation. In both Zion is central and the house of the Lord is to be adorned with splendour, and both are at one that the consequence of Yahweh's intervention will be all that is implied in the word *shālôm*, Isa 60:17; Hag 2:9, namely prosperity and well-being.

The prophet-poet-theologian of chap. 60 is developing traditional theological material out of and into the situation he faced. Verses 7b, 13 indicate that the Temple is not yet standing; v. 10 that the walls are still down; vv. 10, 14, 17 that the people are in a state of subjection; vv. 3-4 that many are still to return to Jerusalem; v. 3 that the nations are still to come. One may date the poem therefore about the time of Haggai and Zechariah 1-8 who date themselves 520 and onwards.

61:1-11.
THE SPIRIT OF YAHWEH IS UPON ME

61 The Spirit of the Lord GOD is upon me,
because the LORD has anointed me
to bring good tidings to the afflicted;
he has sent me to bind up the brokenhearted,
to proclaim liberty to the captives,
and the opening of the prison to those who are bound;
[2]to proclaim the year of the LORD's favour,
and the day of vengeance of our God;
to comfort all who mourn;
[3]to grant to those who mourn in Zion —
to give them a garland instead of ashes,
the oil of gladness instead of mourning,
the mantle of praise instead of a faint spirit;
that they may be called oaks of righteousness,
the planting of the LORD, that he may be glorified.
[4]They shall build up the ancient ruins,
they shall raise up the former devastations;
they shall repair the ruined cities,
the devastations of many generations.

[5]Aliens shall stand and feed your flocks,
foreigners shall be your plowmen and vinedressers;
[6]but you shall be called the priests of the LORD,
men shall speak of you as the ministers of our God;
you shall eat the wealth of the nations,
and in their riches you shall glory.
[7]Instead of your shame you shall have a double portion,
instead of dishonor you shall rejoice in your lot;
therefore in your land you shall possess a double portion;
yours shall be everlasting joy.

[8]For I the LORD love justice,
I hate robbery and wrong;
I will faithfully give them their recompense,
and I will make an everlasting covenant with them.
[9]Their descendants shall be known among the nations,
and their offspring in the midst of the peoples;
all who see them shall acknowledge them,
that they are a people whom the LORD has blessed.

[10]I will greatly rejoice in the LORD,
my soul shall exult in my God;
for he has clothed me with the garments of salvation,
he has covered me with the robe of righteousness,
as a bridegroom decks himself with a garland,
and as a bride adorns herself with her jewels.
[11]For as the earth brings forth its shoots,
and as a garden causes what is sown in it to spring up,
so the Lord GOD will cause righteousness and praise
to spring forth before all the nations.

The prophet speaks in the first person conscious of his mission from Yahweh under the spirit; he is to proclaim salvation, vv. 1-3. He anticipates the consequences and the fulfillment of Yahweh's intervention already begun by the first returns from Babylon and which consists in the complete reversal of the present situation, vv. 4-9. Then, speaking in the name of Zion, he bursts into a hymn of thanksgiving, v. 10, following up with a further assurance that God will be faithful to his word, v. 11. The main motif of the previous chapter are found here, in particular the flow of the wealth of the nations, vv. 6-7, and the glorification of Yahweh in his glorifying Zion.

vv. 1-3. The prophet takes up the words of the first servant song, 42:1, the soliloquy form of the second and third songs as well as the elaboration of the third song in 49:8ff. The spirit of the Lord is upon him inasmuch as he is anointed by Yahweh, an anointing not of the body — this was normally given only to kings and later to the high priest (but see Elijah-Elisha in 1 Kgs 19:15-16, 19) — but a mission, explained by the verb, *to send*, in the second part of v. 1. He, the prophet, and not the watchers as in 40:9; and 52:7, is to bring the good tidings: he is sent "to announce good news . . . to bind up . . . to proclaim . . . to comfort . . . to give . . . ," and all this is to the *'anāwim*, "the poor," v. 1, that is to those whose only resource is God and who do not look to political power or economic status to support themselves; very often they were materially poor; hence to the whole people as in 57:15, and not just to the pious, spiritual few. The prophet is not to proclaim anything new; rather he takes his stand on Second Isaiah and proclaims into the immediate post-exilic situation his message of salvation, *yéshû'lah* and *sedaqah*, which is later guaranteed, v. 11. The words "captives" and "opening of eyes" recall 42:7, but the context is different; those "of a faint spirit," v. 3b, recall "the faintly burning wick" of 42:3. The prophet proclaims further that they are "the oaks of the Just One (*sedeq*), the planting of Yahweh," v. 3cii. The parallelism between *sedeq* and Yahweh indicates that *sedeq* may well be a proper title, the abstract for the concrete.

The opening verses, 1-2ai, are on Jesus' lips when he inaugurates his public mission in the synagogue at Nazareth, Lk 4:16-21, and some commentators have understood them as yet another servant song.

vv. 4-9. As in chap. 60 Yahweh's intervention will bring the nations and their wealth to Zion and the foreigners will work together with the people for the restoration of Zion and Judah, vv. 4-5. The priesthood as a privileged class did not have to engage in agriculture but were entitled to receive from the produce of the labours of those working in the fields. But now the whole people will be a priestly class and benefit from the labours of the nations, vv. 6-7. The Hebrew of v. 6b does not make very good sense. Without any emendation of the text and using a Canaanite parallel, the following is proposed:

> You shall have usufruct of (OR you shall barter with)
> the produce of the nations,
> You shall trade with their wealth.

The Hebrew text of v. 7 is difficult because of the frequent variation between the 2nd and 3rd person plural in verb subjects and pronominal suffixes, variations which differ further in the first Isaiah scroll from the Dead Sea. The RSV emends all five 3rd persons to 2nd persons, which certainly commends itself, though textual evidence is lacking. "For it is I, Yahweh, lover of due order, hater of robbery with violence, who in fidelity will give them their recompense and make an everlasting covenant with them," v. 8. The prophet resumes the words "due order" (*mishpat*) and "recompense" from 49:4 and takes up the theme of everlasting covenant from 55:3. It is Yahweh alone who proclaims and acts, as in Second Isaiah. The fulfillment of the promise made to Abraham of numerous descendants is rooted in the blessing given to him, Gen 12:1-3, and its realization will lead the nations to know that they too shall find their blessing in the truly blessed and chosen people, Gen 12:3; Isa 41:8; 51:2.

vv. 10-11. The proclamation moves into the form of a psalm of thanksgiving, *cf.,* Pss 9:1-4; 30(29):1, and the vocabulary is very like that of v. 3. The prophet speaks in the name of Zion, identifies himself with Zion, who is the object of salvation and righteousness, *yĕsh'uah* and *sedaqah*, of Yahweh's saving action, v. 10a. That Yahweh will do this is as certain as that the cycle of nature will continue, v. 11b, *cf.,*

Gen 8:22. The image of righteousness, *sedaqah*, shooting from the ground is from 45:8.

Some commentators are repelled by what they call the materialism and even greed of chaps. 60 and 62 and want to hear a much more spiritual note in chap. 61, especially as the prophet is proclaiming to the poor and afflicted under the mission of the spirit, v. 1. They tend to "spiritualize" vv. 4-9. But this is to misconstrue the situation. As Gerhard von Rad has written of chap. 60 and Hag 2:6-9:

> It would seem superfluous to say more concerning this text — i.e. with regard to the supposed materialism and avarice which so many expositors have described as a jarring note both in this oracle, and in that of Isa LX. There is no question here of greed for gain, but a proclamation by Yahweh which the prophet set down with uncompromising boldness, and any exegesis which casts doubt upon this mighty purposefulness of Yahweh in the present world-order stands self-condemned in its own supposed spirituality.

When Yahweh intervenes he does so for the total well-being of his people. Chap. 61 stands with chap. 60 and, as we shall see, with chap. 62; the city and Judah are still in ruins, v. 4, and foreigners will be at the service of the people because of God's saving action, already begun in the first returns, and to be fulfilled in his time. We are again in the period not long after the exile and before the rebuilding.

62:1-12. SALVATION COMES TO ZION

62 For Zion's sake I will not keep silent,
and for Jerusalem's sake I will not rest,
Until her vindication goes forth as brightness,
and her salvation as a burning torch.
[2]The nations shall see your vindication,
and all the kings your glory;

and you shall be called by a new name
  which the mouth of the LORD will give.
[3]You shall be a crown of beauty in the hand of the LORD,
  and a royal diadem in the hand of your God.
[4]You shall no more be termed Forsaken,
  and your land shall no more be termed Desolate;
but you shall be called My delight is in her,
  and your land Married;
for the LORD delights in you,
  and your land shall be married.
[5]For as a young man married a virgin,
  so shall your sons marry you,
and as the bridegroom rejoices over the bride,
  so shall your God rejoice over you.
[6]Upon your walls, O Jerusalem,
  I have set watchmen;
all the day and all the night
  they shall never be silent.
You who put the LORD in remembrance,
  take no rest
[7]and give him no rest
  until he establishes Jerusalem
  and makes it a praise in the earth.
[8]The LORD has sworn by his right hand,
  and by his mighty arm;
"I will not again give your grain
  to be food for your enemies,
and foreigners shall not drink your wine
  for which you have labored;
[9]but those who garner it shall eat it
  and praise the LORD,
and those who gather it shall drink it
  in the courts of my sanctuary."
[10]Go through, go through the gates,
  prepare the way for the people;
build up, build up the highway,
  clear it of stones,
  lift up an ensign over the peoples.

[11]Behold, the LORD has proclaimed
to the end of the earth:
Say to the daughter of Zion,
"Behold, your salvation comes;
behold, his reward is with him,
and his recompense before him."
[12]And they shall be called The holy people,
The redeemed of the LORD;
and you shall be called Sought out,
a city not forsaken.

Yahweh's saving action in Jerusalem, equated with Jerusalem's salvation, is the centre of the chapter and is presented under three aspects: 1) the coming of salvation is the coming of Yahweh himself; he is salvation; 2) the salvation is effected before the eyes of the world; 3) the salvation is a grace of Yahweh. The prophet is the speaker and the themes and imagery are from the previous two chapters; he also draws heavily on Second Isaiah. The prophet will not cease to pray and call out until Yahweh's saving action shines forth from Zion and the present desolate situation is reversed, vv. 1-5; the guardians he sets upon the walls will do the same, vv. 6-9; in a string of half-verses and phrases drawn from Second Isaiah he calls the inhabitants of Zion to welcome the final stages of Yahweh's saving action, vv. 10-11. The twelve verses are a continuous prayer for salvation.

vv. 1-5. Yahweh is alleged to have long kept silent and stayed his saving hand, 42:14, 57:11; 64:22; 65:6. Now it is the prophet who will not keep silent until God's saving action and its effects, *sedaqah* and *yĕshû'ah*, v. 1b, shine out like flame from Jerusalem and the nations and their kings see this saving action, *sedeq*, which is God's glory, *kābôd*, his presence among his people, v. 2a; *cf.*, 60:1-3. The presence will give Zion a new name, that is a new status or destiny and it will be Yahweh's gift, vv. 2b-3. This new name is to symbolize the new status: no longer Forsaken, *'ăzûbah* (the name of Jehoshaphat's mother, 1 Kgs 22:42), or Desolate, but "my joy in her" (*Hephzibah*, the name of Manasseh's mother, 2 Kgs 21:1) and "married." The marriage imagery when referred to Yahweh always unites him with his people as a whole. Verse 5aii does not make good sense at all; a slight emendation gives "your builder (i.e. maker of the new city) marries you."

vv. 6-9. Who are the watchmen, or better the guardians? They are the spiritual guardians, conceived as heavenly beings, whom the prophet has appointed. Just as he himself will not keep silent until Yahweh is seen in act, v. 1, so too the guardians will not keep silent day or night, continually reminding Yahweh, giving him no rest, until by his action he makes Jerusalem an object of praise throughout the earth, v. 7. Those who remind Yahweh, the *mazkirim*, are best understood from the term *mazkir*, 2 Sam 8:16; Isa 36:3, a royal official who seems to have been some sort of recorder or official memory, though his function remains obscure. The next two verses, vv. 8-9, describe the future state of the city in the form of a solemn assurance given by Yahweh. For two generations now the farmers have had the frustrating experience of seeing the fruits of their labours go to foreigners; now they shall be able to bring the first born of their cattle and flocks and their tithes of grain, oil and wine in joy to the sanctuary in Jerusalem to celebrate the great feasts, *cf.*, Deut 12:17-18; 14:22-27; 16:9-17.

vv. 10-12. These verses are best seen as a conclusion for chaps. 60-62 in a cluster of passages which the post-exilic prophet draws from Second Isaiah and re-applies within the framework of the immediate post-exilic period. The prophet has been sent under the spirit, 61:1; he is in the prophetic tradition; therefore he can take up and apply the words of a former prophet and master. The double imperatives are typical of Second Isaian style. The addressees are the present inhabitants of Jerusalem who are to throw up a high way, as in 40:3, but in this case outside Jerusalem, to welcome back the people from all lands. The ensign they are to raise is to show these people the way back, v. 10b, whereas the ensign of 49:22 was to be a sign to the nations to bring back the children of Israel. As in Second Isaiah, 42:10; 43:6; 48:20; 49:6, Yahweh's salvation is to be proclaimed to and seen by "the ends of the earth." "Your salvation comes," v. 11b: the Hebrew word is the abstract, *yesha'*, salvation, for the concrete, saviour. Yahweh himself is Israel's salvation; his glory, *kābôd*, 62:2a; 50:1a, 2b, is his presence among them. The last part of v. 11, referring to reward and recompense, is a complete resumption of 40:10a; here the meaning is that Yahweh rewards his people with his saving action. The passage concludes with titles which are familiar from Second Isaiah and with a return to the new name and status of v. 4, Zion shall be Sought Out, Not Forsaken; God has returned to his people.

These three chapters have so much in common in themes, imagery, vocabulary and structure, and reflect virtually the same situation that one can reasonably assign them to the same person. Yahweh's saving intervention and its effects are presented in the following way:

1. Zion is to be established as a great religious centre for all: 60:1-2, 13, 15, 17; 61:10-11; 62:1-2, 7.
2. The wealth of the nations is to flow into Zion: 60:2, 6-7, 17; 61:6-7; 62:2.
3. The nations will take notice of Zion and serve her: 60:10, 14; 61:4, 5, 7, 9; 62:2, 11.
4. The glory and presence of Yahweh shall shine from Zion: 60:1, 7, 9, 13, 17, 19-20; 61:10-11; 62:1-2.
5. Yahweh's saving action and its effects will be experienced: *sedeq*, 61:3; 62:1, 2; *sedaqah*, 60:17; 61:10-11.
6. Salvation will be with them: *yesha'*, 61:10; 62:11; *yěshû'ah*, 60:18; 62:1.

We have already noted points of contact with Haggai and Zechariah 1-8, though there is nothing here of their personal messianism or sense of urgency. Chaps. 60-62 then may be set in the early post-exilic period, round about the same time as these two prophets.

63:1-6.
YAHWEH, WARRIOR AND AVENGER

63 Who is this that comes from Edom,
in crimsoned garments from Bozrah,
he that is glorious in his apparel,
marching in the greatness of his strength?

"It is I, announcing vindication,
mighty to save."

[2]Why is thy apparel red,
and thy garments like his that treads in the wine press?

[3]"I have trodden the wine press alone,
and from the peoples no one was with me;
I trod them in my anger
and trampled them in my wrath;
their lifeblood is sprinkled upon my garments,
and I have stained all my raiment.
[4]For the day of vengeance was in my heart,
and my year of redemption has come.
[5]I looked, but there was no one to help;
I was appalled, but there was no one to uphold;
so my own arm brought me victory,
and my wrath upheld me.
[6]I trod down the peoples in my anger,
I made them drunk in my wrath,
and I poured out their lifeblood on the earth."

What is the form of this extraordinary passage? There is the dramatic use of question and answer as in Cant 3:6; 6:10; 8:5; Ps 24(23):8, 10. More likely however we have the pattern of the watchman or sentry or householder who questions a stranger, who are you? where do you come from? why are you in such a state? It is common in the ancient Near East, in the Homeric epics and in Greek drama. The stranger identifies himself in v. 1c and explains his state in v. 3. He has just come from single combat in which he has devastated his collective enemy. The second part, vv. 4-6, is an elaboration of the first. Verse 5a repeats v. 3a, v. 6a repeats v. 3b.

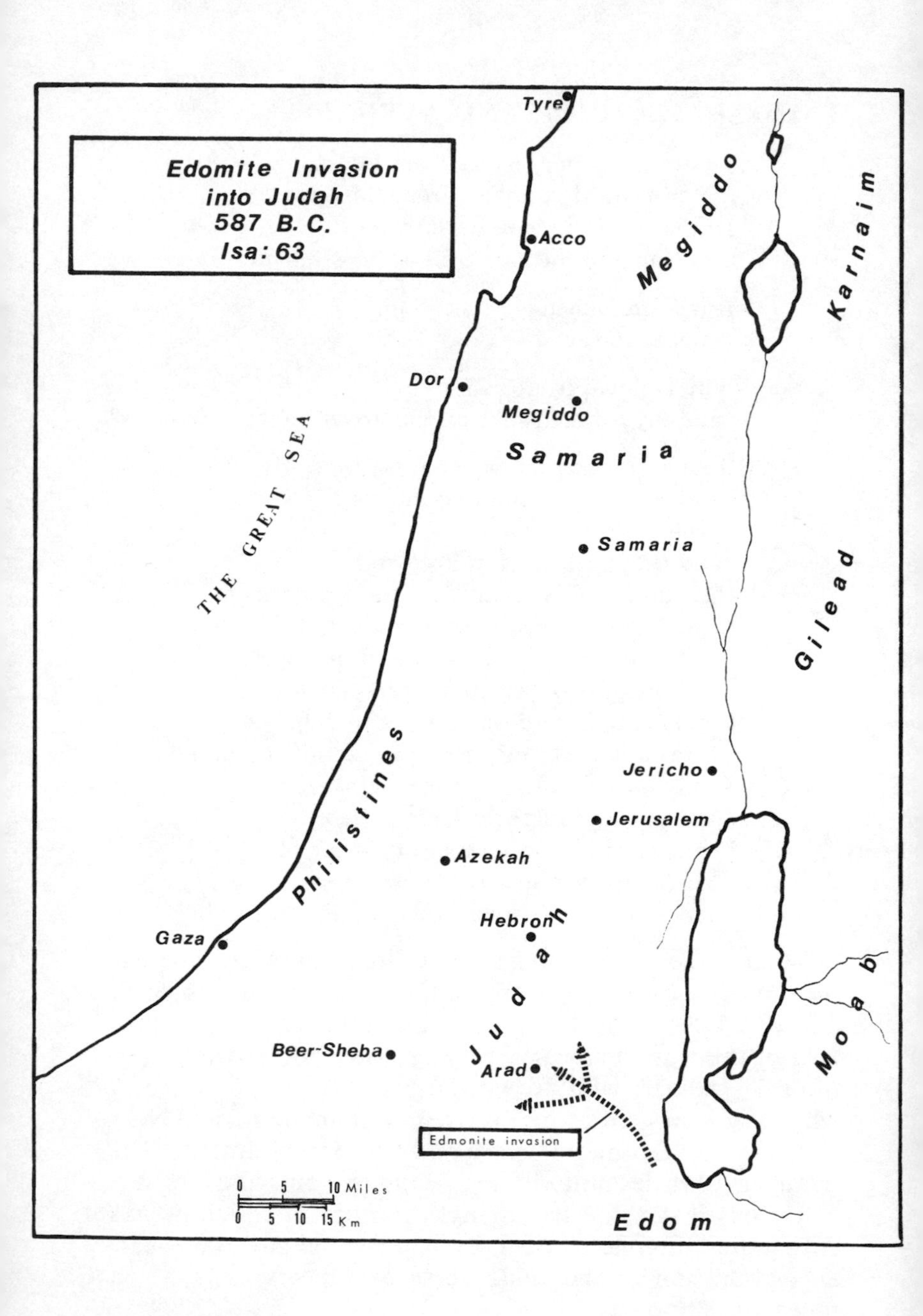
Edomite Invasion
into Judah
587 B.C.
Isa: 63
Tyre
Acco
Dor
Megiddo
Megiddo
Karnaim
Samaria
Samaria
THE GREAT SEA
Gilead
Philistines
Jericho
Jerusalem
Azekah
Hebron
Judah
Gaza
Beer-Sheba
Arad
Moab
Edmonite invasion
0 5 10 Miles
0 5 10 15 Km
Edom

vv. 1-3. This is a highly dramatic presentation of a warrior returning from Edom, the area across the Jordan and south-east of the southern end of the Dead Sea, and its main city, Bozrah, probably the modern Buseira, some 120 miles south of Amman. Judah had had a long history of enmity with Edom going back to the time of David; after the destruction of Jerusalem in 587 Edom had occupied the land as far north as Hebron and had stayed there after the return. This was treachery in the eyes of Judah. There is plenty of biblical evidence for judgment on Edom: Isa 21:11-12; 34:1-17; Obad 1:1-21; Amos 1:11-12; Jer 49:7-22; Ezek 25:12-14; Mal 1:2-5; Joel 4:19; Ps 137(136):7; Lam 4:21-22. The Lord passes gory judgment on Edom and Bozrah in Isa 34:6:

> The Lord has a sword,
> it is sated with blood, it is gorged with fat,
> with the blood of lambs and goats, with the fat of the kidney of rams.
> For the Lord has a sacrifice in Bozrah,
> a great slaughter in the land of Edom.

The word Edom plays on the name of the territory and the colour, red. The anger, wrath and vengeance vented on Edom in Ezek 25:14 is the driving power again in Isa 63 3b, 4a, 6a — the same Hebrew words are used. The garments of the warrior of v. 1 are stained with crimson; he glories in it; he lurches under the weight of his armous and arms. A Canaanite literary prototype of this passage may be the gory lines from the Baal and Anat cycle of Ugarit where Anat returns after crushing her enemies:

> She plunges knee-deep in knights' blood,
> Hip-deep in the gore of heroes.
> (*ANET*, p. 136B, 14-15; 26-30).

The warrior now identifies himself; he makes a stunning self-assertion in the 1st person pronoun, "*'ănî*," "I," familiar from chaps. 40-55; it is Yahweh. The words are a verbal resumption of 45:19c:

I, Yahweh, speaking salvation (*sedeq*),
proclaiming right. 49:19c.
I, speaking out (by means of) vindication
(*sedaqah*), mighty to save. 63:1c.

The images of the wine-press, the wine, blood and stained garments are mingled to the end of v. 6. Lamentations have already described Yahweh in the wine-press, "the Lord has trodden as in a wine-press the virgin daughter of Judah," Lam 1:14. The warrior has fought in single combat, "for from the peoples there was no one with me," v. 3a, *cf.*, 5a. His single-handed victory over Edom stands for his victory over all Israel's enemies.

vv. 4-6. These verses are a loose explanation or elaboration of what has preceded, "indeed, the day of vengeance was in my heart, the year when I took requital has come," v. 4. Then v. 5 almost repeats 59:16:

I stared, and there was no helper,
I was astounded, and there was no supporter;
My right hand saved me, my wrath supported me. 63:5

He looked, no, there was no one,
He was astounded, there was no intervener,
His right hand saved him, his saving action (*sedaqah*)
supported him. 59:16.

This raises the question of the literary relationship between 63:1-6 and 59:15b-21. The following parallels or resumptions may be listed:

59:15b, 16b, 17a	The intervener (warrior) will bring salvation and *sedaqah*	63:1c
59:16	No helper	63:3, 5
59:17b	Day of wrath	63:4
59:20a	Saviour, year of salvation	63:4

Yahweh's coming is imminent in 59:19; his coming is realized in 63:3, 6. All these elements of agreement have led certain exegetes to conclude that the one about to intervene in 59:15b-20 is identical with the warrior and treader of the wine-press of 63:1-6. Some go even further and maintain that the passages belong together and have been separated by chaps. 60-62. However the form and framework of 63:1-6 are different as well as the object of the warrior's action — here Edom and the nations, there Israel herself. Perhaps one could say that Yahweh's salvific action in chaps. 60-62 is flanked by two presentations of his intervention. Judgment is always the other aspect of salvation.

The final verse, v. 6, resumes the image of the grape-treader. To maintain the mingled imagery of battle and the wine-press we may render, somewhat crassly, "I poured their blood-juice on the earth."

What is the passage all about? The mythical background is the god in single combat against the forces of disorder and chaos; the immediate historical background is the enmity between Israel and Edom; the literary background is general Near Eastern, in particular Canaanite and Israelite. It verges on apocalyptic — one man against the nations is beyond all bounds of history; and there may be echoes of the final confrontation with the powers of evil represented in Edom. It is difficult to date and it probably lies outside the bounds of the prophet of chaps. 56-66.

63:7 - 64:12.
A COMMUNAL LAMENT

[7]I will recount the steadfast love of the LORD,
the praises of the LORD,
according to all that the LORD has granted us,
and the great goodness to the house of Israel
which he has granted them according to his mercy,
according to the abundance of his steadfast love.
[8]For he said, Surely they are my people,
sons who will not deal falsely;

and he became their Saviour.
[9]In all their affliction he was afflicted,
and the angel of his presence saved them;
in his love and in his pity he redeemed them;
he lifted them up and carried them all the days of old.

[10]But they rebelled
and grieved his holy Spirit;
therefore he turned to be their enemy,
and himself fought against them.
[11]Then he remembered the days of old,
of Moses his servant.
Where is he who brought up out of the sea
the shepherds of his flock?
Where is he who put in the midst of them
his holy Spirit,
[12]who caused his glorious arm
to go at the right hand of Moses,
who divided the waters before them
to make for himself an everlasting name,
[13]who led them through the depths?
Like a horse in the desert,
they did not stumble.
[14]Like cattle that go down into the valley,
the Spirit of the LORD gave them rest.
So thou didst lead thy people,
to make for thyself a glorious name.

[15]Look down from heaven and see,
from thy holy and glorious habitation.
Where are thy zeal and thy might?
The yearning of thy heart and thy compassion
are withheld from me.
[16]For thou art our Father,
though Abraham does not know us
and Israel does not acknowledge us;
thou, O LORD, art our Father,
our Redeemer from of old is thy name.
[17]O LORD, why dost thou make us err from thy ways

and harden our heart, so that we fear thee not?
Return for the sake of thy servants,
the tribes of thy heritage.
[18]Thy holy people possessed thy sanctuary a little while;
our adversaries have trodden it down.
[19]We have become like those over whom thou hast never ruled,
like those who are not called by thy name

64O that thou wouldst rend the heavens and come down,
that the mountains might quake at thy presence —
[2]as when fire kindles brushwood
and the fire causes water to boil —
to make thy name known to thy adversaries,
and that the nations might tremble at thy presence!
[3]When thou didst terrible things which we looked not for,
thou camest down, the mountains quaked at thy presence.
[4]From of old no one has heard
or perceived by the ear,
no eye has seen a God besides thee,
who works for those who wait for him.
[5]Thou meetest him that joyfully works righteousness,
those that remember thee in thy ways.
Behold, thou wast angry, and we sinned;
in our sins we have been a long time, and shall we be saved?
[6]We have all become like one who is unclean,
and all our righteous deeds are like a polluted garment.
We all fade like a leaf,
and our iniquities, like the wind, take us away.
[7]There is no one that calls upon thy name,
that bestirs himself to take hold of thee;
for thou hast hid thy face from us,
and hast delivered us into the hand of our iniquities.

[8]Yet, O LORD, thou art our Father;
we are the clay, and thou art our potter;
we are all the work of thy hand.

[9]Be not exceedingly angry, O LORD,
and remember not iniquity for ever.
Behold, consider, we are all thy people.
[10]Thy holy cities have become a wilderness,
Zion has become a wilderness,
Jerusalem a desolation.
[11]Our holy and beautiful house,
where our fathers praised thee,
has been burned by fire,
and all our pleasant places have become ruins.
[12]Wilt thou restrain thyself at these things, O LORD?
Wilt thou keep silent, and afflict us sorely?

This communal lament is treated here as a unity. There is 1) the recitation of past blessings, vv. 7-14, 2) the description of the present need and the invocation, 63:15-64:5a, 3) the confession and the appeal for help, 64:5b-7, 4) the confident sense of assurance and the mild admonition to Yahweh, 64:8-12. There are good parallels to this general structure in Pss 44(43); 89(88); 106(105). Ps 44(43) first recalls the history of the exodus vv. 1-2; this is followed by a lament vv. 13-22, and a direct, sharp appeal to Yahweh, "Rouse thyself! Why sleepest thou, O Lord?. . . ." vv. 23-26. The appeal is made on the grounds of Yahweh's steadfast love, *hesed*, v. 26; the grounds for the appeal in Isa 63:16 and 64:8 is that Yahweh is "our father." Ps 89(88) begins, "I will sing of thy steadfast love, (*hesed*), O Lord, for ever. . . . " Then there is the historical narrative and finally the passionate cry to Yahweh, "How long, O Lord? Wilt thou hide thyself for ever? How long will thy wrath burn like a fire?" vv. 46-51. In Ps 106(105) the psalmist begins with some verses of thanksgiving for Yahweh's steadfast love, *hesed*, vv. 1-3, *cf.,* Isa 63:7; there is remembrance of his favours in the past, vv. 4-5, *cf.,* Isa 63:10, and the long recollection of the past history, vv 8-42, *cf.,* Isa 63:11-14. Finally there is a brief cry to Yahweh, "save us, O Lord our God, and gather us from among the nations," v. 47, *cf.,* Isa 63:15-64:12. These parallels are not perfect, but the general analogies are enough to consider the passage a unity with psalm and prophetic motifs mingled together — a commemoration of God's goodness in the form of a hymn, 63:7-14, followed by a lament in which the prophet speaks and the people answer.

vv. 7-14. The first verse of the hymn begins and ends with the word *hesed*, steadfast love, in the plural. The prophet-psalmist will recount, commemorate, actualize God's many acts of love towards his people in the past, *cf.*, Pss 77(76); 78(77); 105(104); 135(134); 136(135). This is no mere mechanical recitation; it is true memorial, the making effective in the present of events in the past. Israel meets its God in history and those great events must be ever present evoking the proper response of praise, that is of acknowledgement that it is God who acts and of real assent thereto with all one's being. Verses 8c-9a may be read better, "He was their saviour from all their affliction, prevailer over the enemy, yes, angel whose presence saved them." It was Yahweh's presence (his face) in his angel (*mal'ak*, messenger) that saved them. "Behold I send an angel before you ....give heed to him and harken to his voice, do not rebel against him, for he will not pardon your transgressions, for my name is in him," Exod 23:20-21. It was the divine presence (the face of God, God's self-manifestation) that brought Israel out of Egypt, Exod 33:41; Deut 4:37. Yahweh's love has always carried them, *cf.*, Isa 46:3. These verses recall the Deuteronomistic pattern of revolt, rebuff, recall, repentance. In v. 11a read "they remembered," and in v. 11b "the shepherd," singular instead of plural. From v. 11b to v. 13 there is a series of five participles of which Yahweh is the active subject, "bringing up," "putting," "causing to go," "dividing," "leading." Verse 14 may be rendered:

> Like a horse in the desert, they did not stumble,
> Like a beast in the broad valley, they did not fall prostrate;
> the spirit of the Lord gave them rest
> (OR Your spirit, O Yahweh, you made rest upon them).

"His holy spirit," vv. 10a and 11c, and "the spirit of the Lord," v. 14a, are unusual. The only equivalent is Ps 51:11. This is the first step on the way to hypostasization which reaches its fulfilment in the Holy Spirit of the New Testament; "to grieve his holy spirit" is picked up in Acts 7:51; Eph 4:30. In Isa 11:2 the spirit of Yahweh will rest upon the chosen one; in Isa 58:11 one may render, "And Yahweh will rest upon you always." The point in the present passage is that it is Yahweh alone who effects his acts of *hesed*.

63:15-64:12. "This psalm is probably the most powerful psalm of lament in the Bible. . . . " (C. Westermann). The passionate prayer that Yahweh turn to the suppliant is addressed to the God who is remote and "so other," but who at the same time has a heart and is compassionate, *cf.,* Exod 34:6f. Yahweh is a living, active, ever present father, not lying in Sheol like the fathers Abraham and Jacob. This address to God as father, together with 64:8 and Deut 32:6, are the only such in the Old Testament and prepare the way for Gal 4:6; Rom 8:15; Matt 6:9. Already in Isa 63:8 the people of Israel are his sons. There follows the accusation against God, v. 17, the complaint about enemies, v. 18, and a lament in the 1st person plural, v. 19. God is one, unique and absolute, therefore he causes everything; Israel, hard of heart, has strayed, therefore God has had a hand in it. It is a question about God, a question of the believer who cannot solve this God-problem, which is also the argument of today's atheist. The Israelite accepts God and will tolerate nothing but the absolute, unique, transcendent one; but the people are perplexed. This hardening of the heart remained always a mystery, but did not in Israel's eyes diminish personal responsibility. The difficulty of v. 18 may be met by rendering "just a little while ago your holy people possessed your sanctuary." The meaning of v. 19 is that the people sense that they are no longer God's possession.

The prayer for God's intervention (64:1-5a) uses the language of a divine epiphany, *i.e.,* of a miraculous appearance of God to deliver his people from a crisis, *cf.,* Judg 5:4f; Ps 18(17):7-15. "Your presense," vv. 1b, 2b, 3b, literally "(confronted) with your face," is the operative phrase. Many authors put v. 4a, "from of old no one has heard," at the end of v. 3a, after "which we looked not for," and read a 1st person plural, "and we have not perceived." The rest of v. 4 still remains difficult and may be read, conjecturally, "no ear has heard, no eye has seen, what God does for those who wait on him." Paul in 1 Cor 2:9 had a text different from the traditional Hebrew. Verse 5 too is difficult; the likely meaning is that God has come upon those whose joy it was to do what they thought proper in following his ways in worship.

Now comes the formal confession of sin 64:5b-7. Again there are difficulties, here in v. 5b. The first part may be rendered satisfactorily, "behold you were angry, and yet we sinned." Then follows literally, "in them of old and we shall be saved." The recent edition of the Hebrew Bible from Stuttgart offers slight emendations and a re-distribution of consonants to give "when you hid yourself we acted wickedly." But this must remain conjectural. All the supposedly righteous deeds of the people are to be cast off definitively; the language is that of ritual uncleanness, Lev 15:19-24. The final cry of despair, v. 7c, is "you have made us melt (*i.e.,* rendered us helpless) because of our iniquities." After the confession comes the turning point, the act of confidence — "but you are our father....," v. 8-12. The emphasis is not on the father-child relationship but on the creator-creature. The people has sinned; God cannot cancel what has happened; yet after all "we are all your people." The lament is resumed in vv. 10-11. The Temple and all its decorations and vessels are in ruins and no more, the very place where praise went up to God is a heap of rubble. Praise was central to the Temple worship; the Temple must be restored so that due praise may go up to God. The lament ends on a somewhat querulous note — surely all is in God's hands.

What is the situation out of which this lament goes up to God? 1) the temple, city and surrounding country are in ruins, 63:18; 64:10-11; hence after 587 and before 515; 2) there is no ruler, they are no longer "called by your name,"

63:19; hence after the collapse of the monarchy and before the new Temple could give them a sense of cohesion; 3) there are enough of them to speak of themselves as "your servants," 63:17b; to think of themselves as "your people," 64:9b; the first group of notable size that could gather around the ruins for a liturgical lament would be shortly after the first major return, in the time of Cambyses or at the beginning of Darius' reign, around 522; 4) the cry is for an intervention from Yahweh, comparable to the Exodus, so that their adversaries might feel it and the nations shake. The psalm then it to be placed well after the destruction of Jerusalem and before the building of the second Temple, when there were sufficient to group themselves together as God's people; it is the reaction of the returned exiles to the ruined city that lay before their eyes. Hence the period 538-520 more or less. We cannot be more precise.

65:1-25.
YAHWEH'S ACCUSATION AND PROMISE

65 I was ready to be sought by those who did not ask for me;
  I was ready to be found by those who did not seek me.
I said, "Here am I, here am I,"
  to a nation that did not call on my name.
[2]I spread out my hands all the day
  to a rebellious people,
who walk in a way that is not good,
  following their own devices;
[3]a people who provoke me
  to my face continually,
sacrificing in gardens
  and burning incense upon bricks;
[4]who sit in tombs,
  and spend the night in secret places;
who eat swine's flesh,
  and broth of abominable things is in their vessels;
[5]who say, "Keep to yourself,
  do not come near me, for I am set apart from you."

These are a smoke in my nostrils,
a fire that burns all the day.
[6]Behold, it is written before me:
"I will not keep silent, but I will repay,
yea, I will repay into their bosom
[7]their iniquities and their fathers' iniquities together,
says the LORD;
because they burned incense upon the mountains
and reviled me upon the hills,
I will measure into their bosom
payment for the former doings."

[8]Thus says the LORD:
"As the wine is found in the cluster,
and they say, 'Do not destroy it,
for there is a blessing in it,'
so I will do for my servants' sake,
and not destroy them all.
[9]I will bring forth descendants from Jacob,
and from Judah inheritors of my mountains;
my chosen shall inherit it,
and my servants shall dwell there.
[10]Sharon shall become a pasture for flocks,
and the Valley of Achor a place for herds to lie down,
for my people who have sought me.
[11]But you who forsake the LORD,
who forget my holy mountain,
who set a table for Fortune
and fill cups of mixed wine for Destiny;
[12]I will destine you to the sword,
and all of you shall bow down to the slaughter;
because, when I called, you did not answer,
when I spoke, you did not listen,
but you did what was evil in my eyes,
and chose what I did not delight in."

[13]Therefore thus says the LORD GOD:
"Behold, my servants shall eat,
but you shall be hungry;

behold, my servants shall drink,
  but you shall be thirsty;
behold, my servants shall rejoice,
  but you shall be put to shame;
[14]behold, my servants shall sing for gladness of heart,
  but you shall cry out for pain of heart,
  and shall wail for anguish of spirit.
[15]You shall leave your name to my chosen for a curse,
  and the Lord GOD will slay you;
  but his servants he will call by a different name.
[16]So that he who blesses himself in the land
  shall bless himself by the God of truth,
and he who takes an oath in the land
  shall swear by the God of truth;
because the former troubles are forgotten
  and are hid from my eyes.

[17]"For behold, I create new heavens
  and a new earth;
and the former things shall not be remembered
  or come into mind.
[18]But be glad and rejoice for ever
  in that which I create;
for behold, I create Jerusalem a rejoicing,
  and her people a joy.
[19]I will rejoice in Jerusalem,
  and be glad in my people;
no more shall be heard in it the sound of weeping
  and the cry of distress.
[20]No more shall there be in it
an infant that lives but a few days,
  or an old man who does not fill out his days,
for the child shall die a hundred years old,
  and the sinner a hundred years old shall be accursed.
[21]They shall build houses and inhabit them;
  they shall plant vineyards and eat their fruit.
[22]They shall not build and another inhabit;
  they shall not plant and another eat;

for like the days of a tree shall the days of my people be,
  and my chosen shall long enjoy the work of their
    hands.
[23]They shall not labor in vain,
  or bear children for calamity;
for they shall be the offspring of the blessed of the
    LORD,
  and their children with them.
[24]Before they call I will answer,
  while they are yet speaking I will hear.
[25]The wolf and the lamb shall feed together,
  the lion shall eat straw like the ox;
  and dust shall be the serpent's food.
They shall not hurt or destroy
  in all my holy mountain,
says the LORD."

A number of commentators think that chap. 65 is an answer to or the logical consequence of the previous passage, 63:7-64:12, while others are of the opinion that there is no connection between the two. Within chap. 65 many would consider vv. 16b-23 to be originally quite separate and to have been joined to the rest by an editor. Be that as it may, the chapter is bound together in vv. 1-2a, 10b, 12b, 24 by the theme of call and answer. Moreover the points of contact between chap. 65 and what precedes are striking:

64:6 There is no-one that calls upon thy name.
65:1b, 24 ...to a nation that did not call on my name.
63:17a O Lord, why dost thou make us err from thy ways and harden our hearts, so that we fear thee not.
64:4b Behold thou wast angry and we sinned; in our sins we have been a long time.
65:2c ...a rebellious people, who walk in a way that is not good, following their desires.

64:11b Wilt thou keep silent and afflict us sorely?
65:6 Behold it is written before me, "I will not keep silent, but I will repay."

64:5b	...our iniquities, like the wind, take us all away...
6d	...and thou hast delivered us because of our iniquities...
65:7	Yea, I will repay into their bosom their iniquities and their fathers' iniquities together...
63:17c	Return for the sake of thy servants, the tribes of thy heritage.
65:8	...so will I do for my servant's sake, and not destroy them all.
9	...my chosen shall inherit it, and my servants shall dwell there.
13-14	(in general, my servants shall be blessed and shall have everything that will make them happy.)

The chapter divides itself naturally beginning with Yahweh's complaint, vv. 1-7, followed by vv. 8-16a which distinguish between "my servants" and "you," and the promise, vv. 17-25. Yahweh is the speaker throughout: there is the complaint, vv. 1-2a, accusation of false worship; vv. 2b-5, and threat of judgment, vv. 6-7. The messenger formula, v.8, introduces a similitude of one verse which contains the reason for the promise; then come promise and threat, vv. 9-10 and vv. 11-12, the two necessary aspects of Yahweh's intervention. The formula occurs again in v. 13 with the particle *lāken*, "therefore," developing in combined promise and threat, vv. 13-16, the promise and threat of vv. 9-12. The introductory formula of vv. 17-25 takes up and develops in detail the general promise of blessing of v. 16. The last verse, v. 25, resumes and actualizes the theme of ideal peace and the holy mountain of Isa 11:6-9. It is a sort of "pesher," a meditation on known texts and an actualization of them.

vv. 1-7. Yahweh has never really been silent, never out of reach of his people. They only have to look for him, to return to him and they will find him. The perverse practices listed in vv. 2b-5 are forbidden cultic rites in which many Israelites have sought Yahweh; they burn incense upon the incense altars (rather than upon bricks) v. 3b, they spend the night in tomb-chambers cut in the slope of the soft rock, v. 4a, a practice known as incubation which looks for an oracle from demons or the dead by passing the night in their presence; they eat swine's flesh, forbidden in Lev 11:7; Deut 14:8, and "the broth of unclean (animals) is their nourishment" (OR "who eat broth out of their vessels"), v. 4b. These Canaanite practices flourished in the monarchic period in both kingdoms, particularly in the reign of king Manasseh (687-642), *cf.*, 2 Kgs 21:1-17, and persevered after the return. Those who practise the rites claim a special holiness for themselves, v. 5a. It is the perennial problem of the first commandment — Yahweh alone is to be worshipped and nothing is to come between creature and creator. The text of vv. 6-7 is somewhat disturbed, but the meaning is clear — all this has been recorded in the heavenly book, and punishment will be meted out where the balance is unfavourable. A last reference to Canaanite ritual practices occurs in v. 7b.

vv. 8-16a. There is division within the Jewish community. There are "my servants" who worship the one true God as is fitting and the "apostates" who seek him, or imagine they seek him, elsewhere. But the whole people will not be discarded because of the wicked; there is still good there. This is the point of the similitude in v. 8. Then the fate of the two groups is spelled out. Jacob and Judah, that is the whole people will be restored; they are "my chosen" and "my servants," the terms applied to the servant in chaps. 40-55. An idyllic scene is portrayed from Sharon, the mountain slope running down to the sea between Mt. Carmel and Joppa in the west, and the valley of Achor near Jericho in the east (Judg 7:24-26; 15:17). Those who forsake Yahweh and his holy mountain, who do not worship him as they ought, will fall by the sword. "Fortune" or "the fortunate one," Gad, in v. 11b, the Greek *tychē*, is well attested in the Phoenician and Palmyrenean inscriptions of Syria in Hellenistic times. But the name occurs also in combination with Baal as the name of a city in Lebanon, Baal-Gad, Josh 11:17; 12:7; 13:5, and as Migdal-Gad in Josh 15:37. "Destiny" is Meni, not otherwise attested, and there is a play on the name in the next verse, "I will destine," by means of the Hebrew verb *mānāh*. Verse 12b makes the obvious link with v. 1, and the phrase "evil in my eyes" is typical of Deuteronomy. In vv. 13-14 there is the heavy contrast between the fate of "my servants" and "you" (the apostates), four times repeated. The mere mention of the name of the inconstant apostates will serve as warning to the true servants, v. 15, and these servants will find their blessing and increase (*cf.*, Gen 12:1-3) in the constant and firm God, literally "the God of Amen."

vv. 16b-25. Verse 16b seems to be a resumption and re-application of 43:18-19. The former things are here specified as the former troubles, that is the events of 587 and the following years. The first word of the Hebrew text *kî* may well be translated by the emphatic "indeed" instead of "because." The next two verses, vv. 17-18, in fact the remainder of the chapter, are dominated by the three times repeated present participle of create, *bārā'*. The salvation to come is announced in vv. 17-19a and expounded in vv. 19b-25. The verses are not in the apocalyptic vein, that is there is not a destruction of the present heaven and earth; rather Yahweh is at work to make Jerusalem new. There will still be death in the new city, but only after life has seen its fulfilment, v. 20. The last part of this verse is better understood as "he who misses the mark of a hundred years...," instead of "the sinner"; "to miss the mark" is the original and literal meaning of the word to sin. The Jewish people did not conceive the ideal life to be a life of idleness but of satisfying work and the enjoyment of the fruits of that work, vv. 21-22a, *cf.*, 62:8. Finally children born into the new Jerusalem will not be confronted with a life of fear and anxiety. Verse 24 takes up and advances vv. 1, 10, 12; Yahweh will anticipate Israel's prayers and invocations; he goes before them and follows them. The last verse resumes in some detail the theme of peace of Isa 11:6-9, setting the scene on "my holy mountain," a phrase used five times in chaps. 56-66. The mysterious hissing of the serpent as it moves along the ground reflects Gen 3:14. All this saving work is accomplished by Yahweh who creates anew as in chaps. 60-62. Once again creation and history are joined.

66:1-24.
ACCUSATION, INTERVENTION, JUDGMENT

66 Thus says the LORD:
"Heaven is my throne
and the earth is my footstool;
what is the house which you would build for me,
and what is the place of my rest?
[2]All these things my hand has made,
and so all these things are mine,
says the LORD.
But this is the man to whom I will look,
he that is humble and contrite in spirit,
and trembles at my word.

[3]"He who slaughters an ox is like him who kills a man;
he who sacrifices a lamb, like him who breaks a dog's neck;
he who presents a cereal offering,
like him who offers swine's blood;
he who makes a memorial offering of frankincense, like
him who blesses an idol.
These have chosen their own ways,
and their soul delights in their abominations;
[4]I also will choose affliction for them,
and bring their fears upon them;
because, when I called, no one answered,
when I spoke they did not listen;
but they did what was evil in my eyes,
and chose that in which I did not delight."

[5]Hear the word of the LORD,
you who tremble at his word:
"Your brethren who hate you
and cast you out for my name's sake

have said, 'Let the LORD be glorified,
that we may see your joy';
but it is they who shall be put to shame.

[6]"Hark, an uproar from the city!
A voice from the temple!
The voice of the LORD,
rendering recompense to his enemies!

[7]"Before she was in labor
she gave birth;
before her pain came upon her
she was delivered of a son.
[8]Who has heard such a thing?
Who has seen such things?
Shall a land be born in one day?
Shall a nation be brought forth in one moment?
For as soon as Zion was in labor
she brought forth her sons.
[9]Shall I bring to the birth and not cause to bring forth?
says the LORD;
shall I, who cause to bring forth, shut the womb?
says your God.

[10]"Rejoice with Jerusalem, and be glad for her,
all you who love her;
rejoice with her in joy,
all you who mourn over her;
[11]that you may suck and be satisfied
with her consoling breasts;
that you may drink deeply with delight
from the abundance of her glory."

[12]For thus says the LORD:
"Behold, I will extend prosperity to her like a river,
and the wealth of the nations like an overflowing stream;
and you shall suck, you shall be carried upon her hip,
and dandled upon her knees.
[13]As one whom his mother comforts,

so I will comfort you;
you shall be comforted in Jerusalem.
[14]You shall see, and your heart shall rejoice;
you bones shall flourish like the grass;
and it shall be known that the hand of the LORD is with his servants,
and his indignation is against his enemies.
[15]"For behold, the LORD will come in fire,
and his chariots like the storm-wind,
to render his anger in fury,
and his rebuke with flames of fire.
[16]For by fire will the LORD execute judgment,
and by his sword, upon all flesh;
and those slain by the LORD shall be many.

[17]"Those who sanctify and purify themselves to go into the gardens, following one in the midst, eating swine's flesh and the abomination and mice, shall come to an end together, says the LORD.

[18]"For I know their works and their thoughts, and I am coming to gather all nations and tongues; and they shall come and shall see my glory, [19]and I will set a sign among them. And from them I will send survivors to the nations, to Tarshish, Put, and Lud, who draw the bow, to Tubal and Javan, to the coastlands afar off, that have not heard my fame or seen my glory; and they shall declare my glory among the nations. [20]And they shall bring all your brethren from all the nations as an offering to the LORD, upon horses, and in chariots, and in litters, and upon mules, and upon dromedaries, to my holy mountain Jerusalem, says the LORD, just as the Israelites bring their cereal offering in a clean vessel to the house of the LORD. [21]And some of them also I will take for priests and for Levites, says the LORD.

[22]"For as the new heavens and the new earth
which I will make
shall remain before me, says the LORD;

so shall your descendants and your name remain.
[23]From new moon to new moon,
and from sabbath to sabbath,
all flesh shall come to worship before me,
says the LORD.

[24]"And they shall go forth and look on the dead bodies of the men that have rebelled against me; for their worm shall not die, their fire shall not be quenched, and they shall be an abhorrence to all flesh."

The final chapter of the oracles gathered under the name of Isaiah is clearly composite. The formulas "(Thus) says Yahweh (OR your God)" and the oracle, *nĕ'um YHWH*, occur eight times in all, though the latter does not necessarily begin or end an oracle. Verses 1-4 go together, despite some difficulties; v. 5 is an isolated oracle; v. 6 "rendering recompense to his enemies" and v. 14 "his indignation is against his enemies" seem to frame Yahweh's definitive intervention in favour of his people, while vv. 15-16 develop the theme of judgment; vv. 17, 18-21 (prose), 22, 23, 24 (prose) are later additions, whether from one and the same hand or from the author of the previous chapters we do not know. At any rate most of these ten verses take up themes already familiar from chaps. 56-66.

vv. 1-4. Some authors set this passage in the middle of the 5th century and understand it as directed against the Samaritans who had not been allowed to join in the building of Zerubbabel's temple in the years 520-515 and now threatened to build their own. But there is no evidence for this opinion in the text. Another view which became one of the main streams of opinion in German scholarship in the last decades of the previous century and the first decades of the present is that the text is an utter rejection of any rebuilding of the Temple. However there is wide agreement now that the verses are meant to counter-balance the view that pervades the two chapters of the prophet Haggai, namely that salvation can come only if the Temple is rebuilt. We read in

Ps 11(10):4, that the Lord's throne is in heaven, and in Pss 99(98):5; 132(131):7, there is a call to worship at his footstool, that is in the Temple. "The humble and submissive of spirit," v. 2b, are typical of the psalms. So vv. 1a and 2b are characteristic of the psalms of praise. Already in Jer 23:24 God had said, "Do I not fill heaven and earth?" And Israel knew very well that God does not need a Temple, as is clear in the promise to David made through Nathan, 2 Sam 7:4-17, and Solomon's prayer at the first dedication: "But will God indeed dwell on earth? Behold, heaven and the highest heaven cannot contain thee; how much less the house which I have built." It is clearly a question of attitude. Yahweh will look to "the one who is humble and submissive of spirit, and trembles at my word," a disposition already underscored in 57:15b; 58:5a; 61:1. The prophetic tradition had constantly condemned an exterior ritual divorced from humble submission to God and justice to the neighbour, *e.g.,* Amos 5:21-23; Mic 6:8. This proper attitude to sacrifice and ritual is well expressed by Roland de Vaux in *Ancient Israel* p. 451:

> Sacrifice is the essential act of external worship. It is prayer which is acted, a symbolic action which expresses both the interior feelings of the person offering it, and God's response to this prayer. . . . it is essential that the external action should express the true inward feelings of man, and that it should be favourably received by God. Failing this, sacrifice is no longer a religious act.

Verse 3a-b is rendered literally:

slaying an ox	striking (killing) a man
sacrificing a lamb	breaking a dog's neck
presenting a cereal offering	(offering) swine's blood
making a memorial offering	blessing an idol

The "like" of the RSV, "who slays an ox is like him who. . .," comes not from the Hebrew but from the Greek and Latin versions. There is a series of eight participles. The first part of each line describes an act of Israelite ritual, the second a Canaanite or Phoenician practice which was an abomination in the eyes of Israel. The passage is best understood as an accusation of syncretism, that is, there were people who were following out both Israelite and pagan ritual — human (child) sacrifice, rites connected with the unclean dog (not otherwise attested in the Old Testament) and pig, and idol worship. Because these people have chosen their own way of worship, Yahweh will choose their affliction, vv. 3c-4.

v. 5. This separate oracle is a word of encouragement to the devout. There is already division in the post-exilic community. Those who stand in awe of the word of the Lord will see their mocking enemies put to shame.

vv. 6, 7-14, 15-16. These verses are best understood as an oracle of salvation, vv. 7-14, framed by a divine epiphany of God coming to pass ultimate judgment on his enemies, vv. 6, 15-16. Yahweh comes from the city and the Temple (presumed rebuilt) to take vengeance, v. 6. The language is traditional with the Hebrew repeating three times the word for voice, *qôl*. The following verses 7-9 take up the image of Zion as mother, *cf.,* 49:18-23; 54:1-3, and give it a different direction. It is the suddenness, omnipotence, miraculous nature of God's action. He will restore his people in an instant, with no painful process. He can do this because he is God.

Salvation as a time of rejoicing pervades the third part of Isaiah, 56:7; 60:15; 61:3, 7, 10; 65:13, 14, 18, 19, as does the like theme of transition from mourning to joy, 60:20; 61; 65:18-19; *cf.,* 49:13; 51:11; 54:1. In the light of recent work on north-west semitic languages the last part of v. 11, after "you may drink deeply," may be read with confidence as "and be filled from her bountiful breast." Verse 12a takes up 48:18, the theme of *shālôm*, the result of God's saving action, and the rest of the verse echoes 60:4. The theme of comfort, and the very word *nḥm*, with which Second Isaiah opens, is resumed and repeated three times in v. 13; the last part of v. 14 catches the Hebrew better when rendered, "the hand of the Lord shall be experienced by his servants, his anger by his enemies." The final verses, vv. 15-16, take up the epiphany of v. 6 and present Yahweh executing apocalyptic judgment on the whole of humankind.

v. 17. This verse turns again to the abominations of 65:3b-5, *cf.,* 57:1-13; 66:3-4. The reference is probably to a revival of condemned cults in the post-exilic period. The words, "following one in the midst," are not clear; mice are regarded as unclean, Lev 11:29. There may be a reference to the sort of rite described in Ezek 8:7-13.

vv. 18-21, 22, 23, 24. The Hebrew text of v. 18a as it stands is unintelligible. The RSV's "know" does not appear in the Hebrew. A number of commentators read "their works and their thoughts" with v. 17 thus giving "their works and their thoughts shall come to an end (perish) together." The Hebrew feminine participle "coming" is read as a masculine, and the first part of v. 19 is read syntactically with v. 18, as in the RSV. Yahweh is speaking; he will gather "all nations and tongues" (Zech 8:23; Dan 3:4; 6:25; 7:29) to Jerusalem and they shall experience his glory in the Temple. We have in vv. 18-21 two movements: in vv. 18-19, 21 a movement outwards to the gentiles, in v. 20 a movement inwards to Jerusalem and its cult; univeralism and particularism are mingled. The sign which Yahweh will set in v. 19a is uncertain; perhaps it is the sending of v. 19b. Some from the nations who have survived the intervention and judgment of Yahweh, who have seen his glory in the Temple, are now sent to make that glory known among the nations; that the nations will acknowledge Yahweh's glory has already been recognized in Second Isaiah and the psalms: "and the glory of the Lord will be revealed, and all flesh shall see it together," 40:5; "and all the ends of the earth shall see the salvation of our God," 52:10; see also Ps 98(97):1-3. The gentiles are sent — the word used in the New Testament for apostolic sending; they are to proclaim by word to their fellow gentiles the glory of God. Tarshish was a Phoenician trading port in the south of Spain, *cf.,* Isa 60:9; Put was in the horn of Africa, Lud also probably in Africa; both occur together in Ezek 27:10; 30:5; the Hebrew consonants and the Septuagint allow us to read Meshek for "who draw the bow"; Meshek and Tubal are south-east of the Black Sea, *cf.,* Ezek 27:13; Javan is the normal Hebrew for the Ionian Greeks along the west coast of Asia Minor. Some of these gentiles, v. 21, are to be fully incorporated into the worshipping people of God as priests and Levites (though there is not unanimity among the commentators that "some of them" in v. 21 refers to the gentiles). But before this comes the particularist v. 20: the gentiles are to bring the scattered of Israel to Jerusalem in solemn ritual procession "as an offering to the Lord," "just as the Israelites bring their cereal offering in a clean vessel..."; the rest of the verse is a resumption of 60:4-9.

Yahweh has renewed the heavens and the earth, *cf.,* 65:17; as they stand firm, so shall the worshipping community, v.22. All flesh, that is all the gentile nations, *cf.,* 40:5, is to take part regularly in the cult, v. 23. Just as the worship is to be everlasting, so too is the judgment, v. 24. The image is of the valley of Hinnom immediately west and south of Jerusalem where the abomination of human sacrifice had been practised, 2 Kgs 23:10; Jer 7:31; 32:35 — the smoking fire and the decaying corpses are ever present. This is the beginning of the description of hell, of everlasting separation from God, resumed and developed in Sir 7:17; Jdt 16:17; Mark 9:43-48; *cf.,* also Enoch 27:2f. There are always two sides to Yahweh's intervention, salvation and judgment.

Some authors insist that v. 24 must be very late because the word "abomination," *dērā'ôn*, occurs elsewhere only in Dan 12:2. But one must be cautious here; words regarded as "late" are often found attested in early tablets or inscriptions in cognate semitic languages, *cf.,* Excursus, *Creation.*

The points of contact with other sections of chaps. 56-66, with Second Isaiah, with Haggai and Zechariah would indicate that vv. 1-16 at least would come from the time of these two prophets; vv. 18-24 could be reasonably set in the same period.

Excursus 4. Sedeq-sedaqah *in Chaps. 56-66.*

The words *sedeq-sedaqah* have almost exactly the same meaning as in chaps. 40-55 and the context is predominantly salvific. *Sedaqah* is very often God's saving act and the well-being and prosperity that accompanies this act, 56:1a; 59:9, 14, 16, 17; 61:10; 63:1; together with 60:17 and 61:11. With *mishpat, sedaqah* is Israel's comportment consequent on the covenant love, 56:1b, 58:2. On two occasions *sedaqah* seems to stand for the true acts of cult which the people should perform as members of a community bound to Yahweh, 57:12; 64:6. *Sedeq* is the prosperity, well-being which belongs to Israel as God's covenant people, the prosperity which comes as a result of God's saving acts, 58:8; 61:3; 62:1, 2. In 58:2 *sedeq* is determined by *mishpat* in the construct plural and the context to mean instructions that will make the people pleasing to God. In 59:4 the meaning is that there is no-one to instruct in such a way as to bring happiness and well-being in accordance with what has been promised. Finally, in 64:5 the word seems to mean acts of cult. *Sedeq-sedaqah* have basically the same meaning, but can have different connotations according to context.

Text	RSV	JB	Comments
56:1a	righteousness	integrity	with *mishpat*; people are to do as they should as God's covenant people
56:1b	deliverance	integrity	with *yeshû'āh*; salvation is near.
57:12	righteousness (ironical)	integrity (ironical)	context of false worship perverse acts of cult.
58:2b	righteousness	integrity	with *mishpat*; what is proper.
58:2c	righteous judgments	laws that are just	the people ask for "ordinances of conduct".
59:9, 14, 16, 17	righteousness(4)	integrity(4)	the whole context is God's saving intervention.
60:17	righteousness	integrity	parallel to *shālôm*; prosperity.
61:3	oaks of righteousness	terebinths of integrity	oaks of the Just One? proper name for God?
61:10, 11	righteousness(2)	integrity(2)	context of joy and prosperity on God's saving action.
62:1-2	vindication(2)	integrity(2)	parallel to *yeshû'āh* and *kabod*; God's presence among his people will blaze before the nations.
63:1	vindication	integrity	parallel to "mighty to save."
64:5, 6	righteousness, righteous deeds	integrity(2)	what the people thought justified them, but were really perverse acts of cult.

FURTHER READING

Commentaries:

J. L. McKenzie, *Second Isaiah* (Anchor Bible 20), New York (Garden City): Doubleday, 1968.

A very fresh interpretation and commentary.

J. Muilenburg, *Isaiah 40-66, Interpreter's Bible 5*, New York (Nashville): Abingdon Press, 1956.

One of the best commentaries on Isaiah 40-66 not only for the theological insights but also for the sensitivity to the rhetorical, poetical and structural qualities.

C. R North, *The Second Isaiah. Introduction, Translation and Commentary to Chapters XL-LV*, Oxford University Press, 1964.

A standard commentary conspicuous for its thoroughness.

C. R. North, *The Suffering Servant in Deutero-Isaiah*, Oxford University Press, 1948 (2nd ed. 1956).

A meticulous study of the history of the exegesis of the servant songs.

C. Westermann, *Isaiah 40-66* (Old Testament Library), London: SCM Press, 1969.

The most recent full commentary; indispensible for an appreciation of the literary forms and the theology of Isaiah 40-66.

R. N. Whybray, Isaiah 40-66 (New Century Bible), London Oliphants, 1975.

A careful philological and theological commentary.

Articles:

Colin G. Kruse, "The Servant Songs: Interpretative Trends Since C. R. North," *Studia Biblica et Theologica* 8(1978) 3-27.

A survey of eighteen articles on the servant songs.

C. Stuhlmueller, "Deutero-Isaiah: Major Transitions in the Prophet's Theology and in Contemporary Scholarship," *Catholic Biblical Quarterly* 42(1980) 3-29.

A survey of recent literature on Isaiah 40-66.

Background References:

J. B. Pritchard (ed.), *Ancient Near Eastern Texts Relating to the Old Testament*, Princeton University Press, 1955 (2nd ed.), *Supplementary Texts*, 1969.

Abbreviated as *ANET*.